A PRACTICAL GUIDE TO INFORMATION LITERACY ASSESSMENT FOR ACADEMIC LIBRARIANS

A PRACTICAL GUIDE TO INFORMATION LITERACY ASSESSMENT FOR ACADEMIC LIBRARIANS

Carolyn J. Radcliff, Mary Lee Jensen,
Joseph A. Salem, Jr.,
Kenneth J. Burhanna, and Julie A. Gedeon

LIBRARIES
UNLIMITED
A Member of the Greenwood Publishing Group

Westport, Connecticut • London

Library of Congress Cataloging-in-Publication Data

A practical guide to information literacy assessment for academic librarians /
  by Carolyn J. Radcliff . . . [et al.].
      p. cm.
   Includes bibliographical references and index.
   ISBN 978–1–59158–340–0 (alk. paper)
     1. Information literacy—Study and teaching (Higher)—Evaluation.
   2. Information literacy—Ability testing. 3. Library orientation for college
   students—Evaluation. 4. Academic libraries—Relations with faculty and
   curriculum. I. Radcliff, Carolyn J., 1961–
   ZA3075.P73   2007
   028.7 071'1—dc22   2007009261

British Library Cataloguing in Publication Data is available.

Library of Congress Catalog Card Number: 2007009261
ISBN: 978–1–59158–340–0

First published in 2007

Libraries Unlimited, 88 Post Road West, Westport, CT 06881
A Member of the Greenwood Publishing Group, Inc.
www.lu.com

Printed in the United States of America

The paper used in this book complies with the
Permanent Paper Standard issued by the National
Information Standards Organization (Z39.48–1984).

10 9 8 7 6 5 4 3 2

To: Taryn, Virginia, Doug, Jon, Peter, Emily, Rick, and
Elaine, with much love.

Contents

Illustrations

Acknowledgments

There are many people who contributed to this book and whose influence is seen in our work. Barbara Schloman provides insightful and highly valued guidance and encouragement in all matters, with healthy doses of down-to-earth advice when needed. Over the years we have collaborated with many clever and dedicated librarians and classroom faculty, and we thank them for their enthusiasm and for inspiring us in our endeavors to effectively teach and assess. We also thank Wendy Torrence and Ryan Wolfe for their indispensable help with this project.

Students are our primary concern and have been the real motivation for writing this book. Helping students become accomplished information seekers and contributors is one of the most rewarding jobs in librarianship and we're proud to play a part.

Part 1

Getting Started

1

Introduction

This book offers practical advice to academic librarians and others who want to ascertain the information literacy levels of their students. It is aimed at practitioners and administrators who need or want to undertake assessment for an entire institution, or for a one-shot instructional session, or something in between.

The book is divided into three sections. In "Getting Started," Chapter 2 presents an overview of the assessment movement in higher education and the role of libraries in that movement. It also describes the three different levels of assessment (classroom, programmatic, and institutional) of most interest to academic librarians. The chapter draws attention to the importance of basing assessment and instruction on clear learning objectives, with guidance for developing or adapting objectives for your own instruction. In Chapter 3, we take you through the book's organization, describing how each chapter is structured and how you can find the best match between your assessment goals and resources and the assessment tools included here.

Nine different assessment tools are covered in the next section titled "The Tools," which is really the heart of the book. You will find in-depth explanations, each with a snapshot of key characteristics, definitions, required resources, and detailed instructions for using the tool successfully, along with examples. Where possible, we include information about applicable online software programs that can help. All these tools have been used in educational assessment for years and most of them have been applied to library assessment as well. By bringing so many tools together in one collection, we hope to draw your attention to tools that are new to you, or show you new uses for familiar tools.

Chapter 4 describes informal assessment techniques, which many of us use all the time but perhaps not to our greatest advantage. Observing, informal questioning, and self-reflection can all be used as immediate feedback to guide our instruction and to identify areas that can benefit from more formalized assessment.

Chapter 5 shows you how several of the classic classroom assessment techniques (CATs) can be applied to information literacy instruction. In clear detail, you will learn how to use these techniques during class so you can make on-the-spot changes if necessary, or provide follow-up information to fill in gaps that the assessment reveals.

Chapter 6 on surveys explains how to construct and administer a survey to understand students' (and perhaps faculty members') perceptions, attitudes, and opinions. With lots of tips on writing good survey questions, guidance on conducting a survey, and some technical advice on the generalizability of results, this chapter will give you a solid grounding in survey methods.

Chapter 7 gives you detailed directions on how to use interviewing as a technique for in-depth exploration of issues with students and faculty. Interviews allow participants to convey their perspectives in their own voices, giving you rich data with which to evaluate instructional programs.

Chapter 8 covers focus groups, which are a good choice for exploring reactions to new programs and for delving into the differences between participants' experiences and outcomes. Focus groups invite student and faculty participants to examine their thoughts and feelings in comparison with the views of others.

Chapter 9 on knowledge tests explains how to write quality objective and essay test questions, using information literacy examples. Learn how to score and analyze results to develop a clear picture of what students know.

Chapter 10 explores the use of concept maps for assessment and instruction, especially in long-term instructional situations. You can use concept maps to guide students' acquisition of new knowledge, and to see in graphic form how students integrate new information into their knowledge bases.

Chapter 11 focuses on performance assessment, which can reveal what students can do. These techniques are a good choice for assessing higher order cognitive skills such as planning, evaluation, and interpretation. The success of this assessment technique relies on good assignment prompts and carefully constructed scoring guides, including checklists, rating scales, or rubrics, all of which are covered in this chapter.

Chapter 12 describes portfolios, an assessment technique that offers extraordinary opportunities for learning how students apply information literacy competencies over time. By systematically examining samples of student work plus the students' self-reflection about their work processes, you can gain useful insights into student learning and application of information literacy skills and concepts.

The third section of the book explains what you can do with the information gathered through the use of the assessment tools. Chapter 13 offers guidance on basic content analysis and simple descriptive statistical techniques. Chapter 14 wraps everything up by describing how to report results effectively to stakeholders, including writing executive summaries and preparing presentations about your assessment. This chapter offers advice on perhaps the most important activity of all—working with the results.

Assessment is essentially meaningless unless you are able to do something with what you learn. Ideally, assessment is part of a continuous process of improvement, as depicted below (see Figure 1.1). As you plan and implement changes, you measure the effect of those changes and make new plans accordingly.

As you read through the chapters, keep in mind some overarching guidelines for the successful use of these assessment techniques:

• Pre-testing. Whether you are writing an assignment prompt, an interview script, survey questions, or knowledge test items, allow yourself enough time to pre-test your work with students. They can let you know if your instructions or questions are confusing, misleading, beyond their understanding, or otherwise not ready.

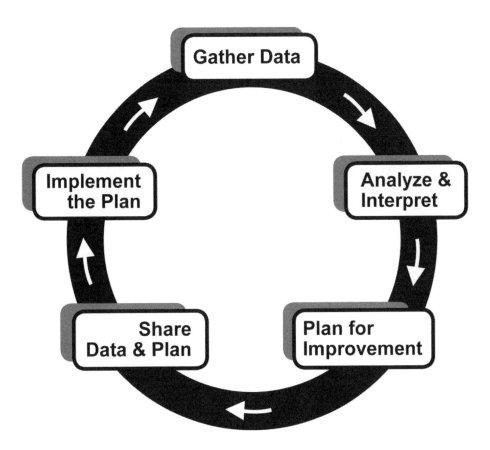

Figure 1.1. The Assessment Cycle.

- Learning objectives. Base your assessment on the learning objectives you have for the instruction. There is little point in measuring student responses to concepts and skills that have not been covered in instruction, unless you want to conduct a pre-assessment.
- Pre-assessment. Very often it is useful to measure students' ability or knowledge before your instructional intervention. Combined with a post-assessment, this allows you to measure change in attitudes, behaviors, or knowledge, which may be more relevant for assessing the impact of your teaching.
- Assessment, not marketing. It can be tempting to use the assessment tool as a marketing or instructional technique. Imagine a survey question: "Did you know that the library offers appointments for students needing in-depth help?" Or picture a focus group leader using the opportunity to spread the word about a new library resource. Avoid this temptation. Promotional efforts dilute the assessment and use up valuable time. There are many other avenues for marketing, so use those instead.
- Follow-through. We simply cannot say it enough—do something with the results of your assessments. Make incremental changes in your instructional technique, share results with library colleagues so that they can consider changes, give feedback to participating students, plan changes to an existing instructional program, collaborate with classroom faculty. Whatever you choose to do will have a positive impact on student learning of information literacy concepts and skills.

If your plans include publishing or making conference presentations about your assessment results, you need to work with your school's institutional review board (IRB). This body oversees research at your institution and is concerned with ethical issues of human participants research. You will have to meet their requirements for conducting research, including maintaining participants' privacy and obtaining their informed consent. We recommend that you get in touch with your IRB early in the process so you have enough time to submit your research request and get approval, which will be needed before you start with the actual assessment.

Whether you are planning to start a systematic program of information literacy assessment at your institution, or simply want some ideas for evaluating the effect of your own instruction, this book will guide you through the assessment process. By offering a selection of tools along with clear directions for using them, we hope to ease the way into regular and effective assessment.

2

A Brief Look at Assessment

Assessment is an integral part of higher education today and is likely to be with us for a long time to come. This situation can be attributed to two major factors. First, at both the state and federal levels there has been increasing emphasis on accountability. Educators in the K-12 system work under mandated grade-level proficiency tests and state standards or guidelines for what should be taught in the curriculum. In higher education, faculty and administrators must respond to accrediting bodies seeking evidence that students are learning or mastering specific competencies. This is true not only for undergraduate programs, but also at the graduate and professional levels.

The second major factor is the growing interest in developing methods of measuring student learning beyond the traditional grading system. This interest stems in part from the trend toward more learner-centered teaching, as well as from an increased focus on lifelong learning. We want to know how we can engage with students, how we can affect their learning, and how we can provide them with the skills they will need after graduation. Assessment plays a role in all of these efforts.

Assessment committees and initiatives abound on college campuses and the "culture of assessment," referring to an environment in which assessment is encouraged, rewarded, and welcomed at all levels, is a term that you may hear frequently. Learning more about what is happening with assessment at your institution will provide you with a framework for your efforts.

WHERE DOES INFORMATION LITERACY FIT IN?

Some colleges and universities have clear-cut expectations for what their students should be able to do upon graduation. These expectations are often referred to as general education requirements or outcomes. For example, a college might expect a student to be able to "interact in a diverse and complex environment" or be a "critical and constructive thinker." At an institution where information literacy is one of the general education outcomes, students might be expected to "use information effectively and responsibly."

If information literacy is a general education requirement, there is an implicit expectation that associated skills will be incorporated into the curriculum and that students will be exposed to information literacy competencies in different ways and at different times throughout their college careers. How information literacy ranks in institutional priorities often depends on whether and how it is included in the institution's mission or strategic plan. Some institutions mention information literacy in their strategic plans, but are not prescriptive about how it is to be included in the curriculum. Others hold departments accountable for assessing the information literacy skills of their students. It is useful for librarians to become familiar with their institution's planning documents and discover where information literacy fits in (if at all).

At a broader level, it is also important to be aware of how information literacy is valued by the associations charged with accrediting your college or university. There are six regional accrediting bodies (see Figure 2.1 for a list of these and a sample of other accrediting agencies) and the inclusion of information literacy varies considerably from one agency to another. For example, as part of its accrediting process, the Middle States Commission on Higher Education (2003) looks for evidence that information literacy skills are integrated within an institution's curriculum. The Commission strongly encourages colleges and universities to place a high importance on information literacy in their strategic planning and in their assessment of student learning. This sets the stage for librarians to provide leadership on campus and to work collaboratively with faculty and administrators on information literacy initiatives.

In contrast, the Higher Learning Commission of the North Central Association does not have specific information literacy requirements. Instead, the focus is on institutional priorities, regular assessment, and steady improvement. Since 1999 the Commission has encouraged member institutions to adopt the Academic Quality Improvement Project (AQIP; www.aqip.org) assessment process. AQIP focuses on continuous improvement and requires institutions to submit a self-assessment as a first step in developing action plans. Because each college or university identifies unique areas in which improvement is needed, information literacy assessment may or may not be included in the institutional action plan. In this setting, librarians may need to be more persuasive in pursuing and promoting information literacy as an institutional goal.

Accreditation guidelines change over time, in the same way institutional priorities change. It is important not only to know whether information literacy is currently included, but also to monitor initiatives that may be underway. Being aware of how information literacy is valued by the accrediting body for your college or university will also provide you with a foundation for discussions with faculty and administrators.

WHERE DO LIBRARIES FIT IN?

The very act of engaging in assessment implies that there are standards against which a body of work, a performance, or a set of skills can be measured. For example, gymnastics judges rely on their own experience as well as standards within the sport to identify what constitutes a perfect performance on the balance beam or a 10 on the vault, and gymnasts are assessed based on those standards of perfection.

As librarians, we use our own research experiences, our knowledge of the literature, and our observations and interactions with students to help us form a definition of an information literate person. Like observing a perfect back flip, we know it when we see it (and when we don't). We also rely on criteria developed by our own professional

Organizations acting as accrediting bodies are recognized by the United States Department of Education (http://ope.ed.gov/accreditation/) and/or by the Council for Higher Education Accreditation, a nongovernmental organization (www.chea.org).

Regional Accrediting Organizations:

- Middle States Association of Schools and Colleges
  Commission on Higher Education (www.msche.org)
     Delaware, Maryland, New Jersey, New York, Pennsylvania, Puerto Rico, U.S. Virgin Islands, Washington D.C.

- New England Association of Schools and Colleges
  Commission on Institutions of Higher Education (www.neasc.org/cihe/cihe.htm)
     Connecticut, Maine, Massachusetts, New Hampshire, Rhode Island, Vermont

- North Central Association of Colleges and Schools
  Commission on Institutions of Higher Education (www.ncacihe.org)
     Arizona, Arkansas, Colorado, Illinois, Indiana, Iowa, Kansas, Michigan, Minnesota, Missouri, Nebraska, New Mexico, North Dakota, Ohio, Oklahoma, South Dakota, West Virginia, Wisconsin, Wyoming

- Northwest Commission on Colleges and Universities (www.nwccu.org)
     Idaho, Montana, Nevada, Oregon, Washington, Utah

- Southern Association of Colleges and Schools
  Commission on Colleges (www.sacs.org)
     Alabama, Florida, Georgia, Kentucky, Louisiana, Mississippi, North Carolina, South Carolina, Tennessee, Texas, Virginia

- Western Association of Schools and Colleges
  Accrediting Commission for Community and Junior Colleges (www.accjc.org)
  Accrediting Commission for Senior Colleges and Universities
  (www.wascsenior.org/wasc/)
     California, Guam, Hawaii

National Accrediting Organizations

     Accrediting Commission of the Distance Education and Training Council
     Accrediting Council for Independent Colleges and Schools
     Association for Biblical Higher Education Commission on Accreditation

Specialized and Professional Accrediting Organizations

There are more than 70 organizations that fall in this category. Here are a few:
     American Dietetic Association
     American Physical Therapy Association
     American Psychological Association Commission on Education
     American Society of Landscape Architects
     Commission on Accreditation of Allied Health Education Programs
     Council on Social Work Education
     National Council for Accreditation of Teacher Education

Figure 2.1. Accrediting Organizations.

associations. For example, in 2000 the Association of College and Research Libraries (ACRL) developed *Information Literacy Competency Standards for Higher Education: Standards, Performance Indicators, and Outcomes* (2000). (See Figure 2.2.) In 2001, ACRL adopted the *Objectives for Information Literacy Instruction: A Model Statement for Academic Librarians*, which breaks down the standards into distinct and measurable components so that they can be used when planning instruction. Both the standards and objectives can be used together as a framework for classroom, programmatic, and institutional assessment. Anyone doing information literacy assessment in higher education is encouraged to start by examining the extensive resources available through the ACRL Web site on information literacy (www.ala.org/ala/acrl/acrlstandards/informationliteracycompetency.htm).

The ACRL standards are not, however, the only information literacy competencies available to you. Some colleges and universities have adapted the standards or developed their own set of competencies for their students (see Figure 2.3). Take advantage of existing models and use them as appropriate in conjunction with your own instructional goals to form the foundation of your assessment planning.

Throughout the planning process and as you proceed with efforts to promote information literacy assessment, it is important to remember that faculty may not be aware of the library standards that have been developed either through ACRL or at other universities. Even if they are tuned in, they may be resistant to having guidelines imposed from another discipline onto their own. Their perceptions of information literacy stem from their own experiences as both teachers and researchers and are based in their disciplines.

To gain a faculty member's willing cooperation with your assessment efforts, it is critical to come to a common understanding of how you both define information literacy,

---

Standard One: The information literate student determines the nature and extent of the information needed.

Standard Two: The information literate student accesses needed information effectively and efficiently.

Standard Three: The information literate student evaluates information and its sources critically and incorporates selected information into his or her knowledge base and value system.

Standard Four: The information literate student, individually or as a member of a group, uses information effectively to accomplish a specific purpose.

Standard Five: The information literate student understands many of the economic, legal, and social issues surrounding the use of information and accesses and uses information ethically and legally.

Each of the standards incorporates detailed performance indicators and outcomes that can be used in developing assessment projects.

Figure 2.2. Information Literacy Competency Standards for Higher Education.

Source: Association of College and Research Libraries (ACRL). (2000). *Information literacy competency standards for higher education: Standards, performance indicators, and outcomes.* Retrieved May 23, 2006 from www.ala.org/ala/acrl/acrlstandards/informationliteracycompetency.htm.

Colgate University (2004): The libraries established a mission, goals, and accompanying detailed objectives related to information literacy skills for first year students and for graduates. http://exlibris.colgate.edu/InformationLiteracy/mission.html.

Florida International University Libraries (2002): Developed a mission statement, goals, and objectives for information literacy following the establishment of an information literacy requirement in 1998. The *Web site* also includes library instruction outcomes for specific courses. www.fiu.edu/~library/ili/

Indiana University (1996): Adopted 9 basic goals as part of its assessment plan for information literacy. www.indiana.edu/~libinstr/Information_Literacy/assessment.html.

University of Louisville Libraries (2001): Provides a model for how the ACRL learning outcomes can be applied to specific courses. http://library.louisville.edu/infoliteracy/outcomes.html.

Wisconsin Association of Academic Librarians (1998): Established a framework of 10 competencies to describe an information literate student. www.wla.lib.wi.us/waal/infolit/ilcc.html.

Figure 2.3. Sample of Information Literacy Standards Developed at Colleges and Universities.

as well as the goals for student learning and assessment. This can be accomplished through informal conversations, departmental meetings, or workshops. Depending on the culture of your institution, you might also want to consider hosting a lecture by an external expert on information literacy assessment, with follow-up discussion among librarians and classroom faculty.

LEVELS OF ASSESSMENT

Engaging in information literacy assessment allows us to quantify our perceptions so that we are prepared to have meaningful conversations with faculty and administrators. It helps us determine whether our instruction makes a difference in the acquisition and retention of information literacy skills. And it assists us in identifying gaps in our instruction and informing us as to what we can do to improve our instruction.

Assessment can be done at three different levels: classroom, programmatic, and institutional. The level of assessment in which you engage will be dependent on many factors, most particularly time, resources, and access to faculty. Each will provide you with unique information about students' information literacy competencies. As noted in a report by the Middle States Commission on Higher Education, "One advantage of assessing at multiple levels of the organization is that it provides comprehensive data for understanding how student learning is taking place so that the teaching and learning process can be improved" (2003, p. 44). Read on for a brief description of the three levels.

Classroom Assessment

Classroom assessment is sometimes referred to as course assessment. Assessment done at this level allows for more direct feedback about student learning as it relates to a specific class period or several class periods throughout a semester. It focuses on one course at a time and is tied to course or class learning objectives. Librarians are most likely to be involved in classroom assessment because our access to students is often limited to one class. Classroom assessment is both manageable and requires the fewest number of resources. Many of the assessment tools highlighted in this book focus on classroom assessment.

Programmatic Assessment

Programmatic assessment is more focused than institutional assessment. As its name implies, it centers on the learning goals for a program of study or a series of courses that comprise a program. This is where the information literacy standards promoted by a particular profession or discipline (for example, nursing, teacher education, or social work) enter the picture. See Figure 2.4 for an example of how one librarian used accrediting criteria and assessment to facilitate information literacy integration.

A librarian tells this story about how accrediting criteria and assessment can affect the integration of information literacy:

In the late 1990s, I worked in a branch library of a mid-size research university. My library supported the needs of students obtaining master's and doctoral degrees in social work. For several years I worked with colleagues to institute a plan that would orient students to library resources and then build on that mandatory orientation by teaching specific information literacy competencies in prescribed courses. Although this worked well for full-time students, the school had a large number of students who took courses only on the weekends. Their orientation and subsequent instruction was more haphazard, although these were usually the students who needed the information literacy skills more (especially assistance with electronic resources) because they tended to be non-traditional students.

One year, the program came up for accreditation by the Council on Social Work Education (CSWE). At one particular curriculum committee meeting, I presented data to faculty and administrators on the instruction that students were receiving by type of student. I had done a simple pre- and post-test relating to students' knowledge and use of particular databases (before and after instruction) and the data showed the value of information literacy instruction, at least in this context.

At the time, one of the mandates for accreditation from CSWE was that all populations of students in a program receive equivalent instruction. Members of the administration realized that the weekend students were receiving less instruction than the full-time students and that they were not performing as well on the post-test. As a result, there was unanimous support for the expansion of the library orientation and instruction program for the weekend students, which allowed us access to the students we wanted to reach and created a more uniform instruction program. Without the clout of an accreditation emphasis on equivalent services, this program development might not have occurred.

Figure 2.4. Using Accreditation Standards to Foster Assessment: One Librarian's Story.

Keep in mind that standards for professional associations may be different from those adopted at the institutional level. For example, an institution's overall accrediting body or strategic plan may designate information literacy as a low priority, but an academic department's accrediting organization may consider information literacy to be very important.

Programmatic assessment usually involves targeting specific academic departments and working closely with the department chair and the faculty to integrate information literacy instruction and related assessment. When you are involved in programmatic assessment, you are more likely to measure progress over a period of time within a discipline.

Institutional Assessment

Institutional assessment provides a broad overview of students' information literacy skills; its goal is to look across departments and disciplines. Assessment of information literacy at an institutional level focuses on what skills the student body as a whole possesses. It may involve assessing students as they enter the university and again in their last year. Or, it may compare departments to gauge whether the degree of instruction in different programs affects student knowledge of information literacy competencies. Institutional assessment requires a high level of commitment, both in terms of time and resources. If you intend to embark on information literacy assessment at this level, it is important for you to identify key players and departments on campus who can assist you. You will need both their cooperation and their expertise.

Begin by finding out whether there is an assessment officer on your campus—someone charged with reporting data to accrediting bodies or coordinating assessment initiatives. Become familiar with the accreditation procedures on your campus and within departments. Collect information on assessment committees, current and past. Depending on the size of your institution, you might consider using a faculty e-mail discussion list to collect this information or to identify those on campus who have an interest in assessment. Your chances for carrying out meaningful information literacy assessment at your institution will increase if there is campus dialogue around the issue. To facilitate discussion, it helps to be familiar with assessment terminology. Figure 2.5 offers four fundamental definitions.

Even if you are not planning on doing institutional assessment, it is still helpful to gather data on the kind of information literacy instruction that is carried out on your campus. You may want to survey faculty as to how they address information literacy competencies in their classrooms. If your institution designates courses as fulfilling writing requirements, collecting a list of such courses can provide you with leads as to where information literacy is more likely to be taught and where it might be assessed.

Depending on the size of your library, you may also want to do some data gathering on your home turf about information literacy instruction. If you work in a library where only one or two librarians are responsible for information literacy instruction, you can probably summarize the instruction that is underway fairly easily. If, however, you work in a library where ten or more librarians are doing information literacy outreach, it may first be necessary to gather data internally about the kind of skills that are being taught by different librarians and at what level. You may be surprised at what you find!

This groundwork (establishing contacts, gathering data and information) can help you develop priorities for assessment and will assist in planning efforts.

Formative assessment

Formative = in process; progress along the way; developmental.

Examples: Classroom assessment techniques; in-class exercises; reflections on the process of learning.

Formative assessment can be conducted while students are learning in order to gauge what they are learning. It can provide valuable feedback that can be used to improve instruction.

Summative assessment

Summative = the final result; adding pieces of information together to get a sum.

Examples: Final exams; surveys at the end of courses; exit surveys as students graduate; reflective components of portfolios summarizing the value of a project.

Summative assessment can be used to determine whether learning outcomes or information literacy competencies have been met or mastered.

Direct or authentic assessment

Characterizes assessment that is a result of direct contact with a student. This could be a product, such as a search strategy developed by a student in class, or a portfolio of student work. It also includes tests, annotated bibliographies, and papers.

Indirect assessment

Characterizes assessment information that has been inferred from observation or from surveys. It is subject to interpretation and relies on inferences.

Figure 2.5. Some Key Assessment Terms.

LEARNING OBJECTIVES

Regardless of the level at which you are assessing—classroom, programmatic, or institutional—assessment should be clearly aligned to your objectives for student learning. A learning objective is a statement of what you want students to learn as a result of a learning experience, such as a library instruction session. Learning objectives should fit within the larger context of the course objectives, departmental goals, or institutional priorities. Ideally, learning objectives are measurable, which greatly facilitates assessment. For most library instruction, which typically consists of one or two sessions per class, it is generally agreed that limiting instruction to two or three learning objectives per session is best. You may find this difficult to do, especially if you feel pressure to teach the students "everything they will need to know" because this could be your only chance. By focusing your instruction on only a few objectives, however, you will find that you actually have enough time to cover the material thoroughly, your students will not be as overwhelmed, and you may find that more learning is taking place.

Having learning objectives that are well-defined for each instructional session is good practice and makes assessment easier. Learning objectives help you focus on what to teach and what to assess. Although this might seem obvious, there are many instances in which we fail to teach students the skills that we want them to have. For example, imagine an instruction session in which you demonstrate how to do a search in a database. You do not explain the exact role of Boolean operators in your examples, yet your end-of-class quiz includes questions on their proper use. When you analyze the results, you may be surprised to see that students did poorly on the concept, only to realize that you had neglected to give it weight during your instruction—even though you thought it was important enough to include on the quiz. You can avoid this type of situation by writing and using learning objectives for each session.

There are many approaches for writing learning objectives and many helpful resources, such as Norman Gronlund's book, *Writing Instructional Objectives for Teaching and Assessment* (2004) and Linda Suskie's chapter on learning goals in her book, *Assessing Student Learning: A Common Sense Guide* (2004). Both sources give context, explain the process, and offer examples, though not for library or information literacy instruction. Gronlund's work in particular provides detailed, valuable guidance in a clear and approachable style. It is aimed at K-12 practitioners but much is applicable to the higher education environment.

Another approach to writing learning objectives was introduced by Heinich and his colleagues in their work, *Instructional Media and Technologies for Learning* (Heinich, Molenda, Russell, and Smaldino, 2002). In the "A-B-C-D" method, every learning objective should address four aspects:

A is for audience, the intended learners;
B is for behavior, what you expect the learner to do;
C is for conditions, the circumstances under which the learning will occur;
D is for degree, or how much of the behavior needs to be performed and to what level.

Figure 2.6 has examples of information literacy learning objectives developed with the A-B-C-D method. As you read them, notice how unambiguous and measurable each objective is. If we wanted to assess how well the objectives were met, we would have clear direction for doing so.

Another very well-known approach to learning objectives is the taxonomy of educational objectives first published by Benjamin Bloom in 1956. In the taxonomy, the

---

After explanation and an example (C), students (A) will be able to identify the major concepts that make up their research topics (B), as determined by librarian examination of student work (D).

Through a group exercise to construct a list of the characteristics of scholarly, professional, and popular periodicals (C), students (A) will be able to identify which category a particular periodical issue falls into (B), with 80% of students able to correctly choose the category (D).

After receiving instruction that explains the value of reference books and *Access Science*, the online *McGraw-Hill Encyclopedia of Science and Technology* (C), 75% (D) of students in the Biodiversity Lab course (A) will include a reference book in their list of citations for their oral report topic (B).

Figure 2.6. Examples of Information Literacy Objectives that Follow the A-B-C-D Method.

domains of learning are:

> Affective: What are students' perceptions and values?
> Behavioral: What can students do?
> Cognitive: What do students know?

We use these domains throughout this book to identify which assessment tools are appropriate to your learning objectives. You can read more about that in the next chapter, "How to Choose the Right Assessment Tool."

Bloom's taxonomy and subsequent revisions (see Anderson and Krathwohl, 2001) can give you quite a detailed and thorough look at the processes of teaching and learning. They offer a wealth of ideas for formulating learning objectives, particularly in the cognitive domain. Within the cognitive domain, there are six levels of cognitive complexity. From lower to higher, they are:

- *Remember*: Retrieve relevant knowledge from long-term memory.
- *Understand*: Construct meaning from instructional messages, including oral, written, and graphic communication.
- *Apply*: Carry out or use a procedure in a given situation.
- *Analyze*: Break material into its constituent parts and determine how the parts relate to one another and to an overall structure or purpose.
- *Evaluate*: Make judgments based on criteria and standards.
- *Create*: Put elements together to form a coherent or functional whole; reorganize elements into a new pattern or structure (Anderson and Krathwohl, 2001, pp. 67–68).

Teachers and librarians have used the taxonomy extensively to write learning objectives and to place objectives along the domains. Anderson and Krathwohl's book (2001), like Bloom's original publication, offers scores of verbs that can help you write objectives. For example, if you want students to learn something at the *Analyze* level, you might choose one of these verbs to start things off: analyze, distinguish, subdivide, design, illustrate, utilize, categorize, identify, survey, detect, outline, classify, infer, arrange, diagram, relate, compare, break down, develop, point out, differentiate, select, combine, discriminate, separate. Taking advantage of this list, an information literacy objective at the *Analyze* level might read:

Students will **illustrate** the publication cycle of scholarly articles by making a flow chart.

The taxonomy developed by Anderson and Krathwohl has two dimensions. You have already read about the cognitive complexity dimension; the other dimension is knowledge, of which there are four types:

- factual knowledge;
- conceptual knowledge;
- procedural knowledge;
- meta-cognitive knowledge.

Anderson and Krathwohl (2001) advocate a holistic approach to teaching and assessment using both dimensions of the taxonomy table. In their model, the learning objective, teaching method, and assessment technique should all be at the same cognitive level and should all address the same type of knowledge. For instance, let's say you want students to understand how scholarly articles get published. You develop a learning objective like the one above, which requires students to *analyze conceptual knowledge*. To make your instruction focus on analyzing conceptual knowledge, you decide to teach the steps in the publication cycle for one discipline, say, the social sciences. You show students how original research carried out for a dissertation can be presented at a conference, and eventually work its way through the peer review process to publication. Your instruction helps students to see how these steps relate to the larger academic publication process.

After your instruction, you give students an assessment task that draws them into making connections between the parts of the system and the larger whole (conceptual knowledge). One way of doing this is to provide students cards with a different component of the publication cycle on each one. Students can use the cards as prompts to make a flow chart of how scholarly articles might be published in a different discipline (for instance, the sciences). In this way, the assessment echoes the cognitive level and knowledge type of the instruction and students are able to fulfill the learning objective.

As mentioned earlier in this chapter, you may wish to turn to ACRL for ready-made objectives that can be selected or adapted for your own instructional goals and settings. When you review the ACRL objectives, you will see that they start with verbs in a manner similar to Bloom's taxonomy and the revision by Anderson and Krathwohl, such as: determines, assesses, selects, uses, identifies, evaluates, retrieves, demonstrates, locates, investigates, realizes. See Figure 2.7 for examples.

Writing objectives can seem overwhelming at first. The good news is that there are many models you can follow. You can also start with a simple framework and build your objectives as you gain more experience and as you become more familiar with the literature on learning objectives. Just remember, no matter what method you use to write your objectives, keep them to a minimum so that you can adequately cover the material. This will insure that the assessment you do is directly correlated to the teaching that you have done.

Now that you have some background on assessment, we encourage you to read on and learn more about appropriate assessment tools. The next chapter will describe key indicators of assessment tools and guide you through deciding which tools are appropriate for your situation and goals.

- Describes the publication cycle appropriate to the discipline of a research topic.
- Defines the "invisible college" (e.g., personal contacts, listservs specific to a discipline or subject) and describes its value.
- Demonstrates an understanding of the concept of truncation and uses it appropriately and effectively.
- Identifies citation elements for information sources in different formats (e.g., book, article, television program, Web page, interview).

Figure 2.7. Examples of ACRL Objectives.

Source: Association of College and Research Libraries (ACRL). (2001). *Objectives for information literacy instruction: A model statement for academic librarians*. Retrieved May 23, 2006 from www.ala.org/ala/acrl/acrlstandards/objectivesinformation.htm.

WORKS CITED AND FURTHER READING

Anderson, L. W. and Krathwohl, D. (Eds.). (2001). *A taxonomy for learning, teaching, and assessing: A revision of Bloom's taxonomy of educational objectives*. New York: Longman.

Association of College and Research Libraries (ACRL). (2000). *Information literacy competency standards for higher education: Standards, performance indicators, and outcomes*. Retrieved May 23, 2006 from www.ala.org/ala/acrl/acrlstandards/informationliteracycompetency.htm.

Association of College and Research Libraries (ACRL). (2001). *Objectives for information literacy instruction: A model statement for academic librarians*. Retrieved May 23, 2006 from www.ala.org/ala/acrl/acrlstandards/objectivesinformation.htm.

Bloom, B. S. (Ed.). (1956). *Taxonomy of educational objectives: The classification of educational goals*. New York: D. McKay Co., Inc.

Clark, D. (2001). *Learning domains or Bloom's taxonomy*. Retrieved July 10, 2006 from http://www.nwlink.com/~donclark/hrd/bloom.html.

Cruz, E. (2003). Bloom's revised taxonomy. In B. Hoffman (Ed.), *Encyclopedia of educational technology*. San Diego, CA: San Diego State University Department of Educational Technology. Retrieved July 10, 2006 from http://coe.sdsu.edu/eet/Articles/bloomrev/index.htm.

Gronlund, N. E. (2004). *Writing instructional objectives for teaching and assessment* (7th ed.). Upper Saddle River, NJ: Pearson/Merrill/Prentice Hall.

Heinich, R., Molenda, M., Russell, J. D., and Smaldino, S. E. (2002). *Instructional media and technologies for learning* (7th ed.). Upper Saddle River, NJ: Merrill/Prentice Hall.

Hernon, P., Dugan, R. E., and Schwartz, C. (2006). *Revisiting outcomes assessment in higher education*. Westport, CT: Libraries Unlimited.

The Higher Learning Commission. (2006). *Academic quality improvement program*. Retrieved May 23, 2006 from www.aqip.org.

Middle States Commission on Higher Education. (2003). *Developing research and communication skills: Guidelines for information literacy in the curriculum*. Philadelphia, PA: Middle State Commission.

Neely, T. Y. (2006). *Information literacy assessment: Standards-based tools and assignments*. Chicago, IL: American Library Association.

Saunders, L. (2007). Regional accreditation organizations' treatment of information literacy: Definitions, collaboration, and assessment. *Journal of Academic Librarianship*. In press.

Suskie, L. A. (2004). Developing learning goals. *Assessing student learning: A common sense guide*. Bolton, MA: Anker Publishing (pp. 73–93).

3

How to Choose the Right Assessment Tool

Now that you have some background information on information literacy assessment, it is time to learn more about the tools available to you. As you read through the material in this book, you will find that some tools work better for certain kinds of assessment than others. For example, recall the three levels of assessment described in Chapter 2: classroom, programmatic, and institutional. The level that you are assessing can be a key factor in your choice of tools. Another way to categorize the tools is by learning domain, also described in Chapter 2. To determine the domain that interests you, ask yourself whether you want to assess how students feel or their opinions (affective domain), what students can do (behavioral domain), or what students know (cognitive domain). Then choose tools that measure in that domain.

Figure 3.1 is a quick guide that classifies the assessment tools in this book by both the level of assessment and the assessment domain. As you will see, some tools can be used at multiple levels and can assess multiple domains. The tool you choose also has much to do with your comfort level in using it, and by the amount of available time and money. To make a more thoughtful decision about which assessment tool to use, we suggest that you read the descriptions provided in Chapters 4 through 12. The next section provides you with an overview of how each chapter is organized.

CHAPTER ORGANIZATION

Chapters 4 through 12 describe the individual tools. Each begins with a set of icons representing seven key indicators: time, money, level, domain, access to participants, degree of faculty collaboration, and need for outside expertise. Here is a description of the icons:

	Classroom	**Programmatic**	**Institutional**
Affective	Informal (Chapter 4) CATs (Chapter 5) Surveys (Chapter 6) Portfolios (Chapter 12)	Surveys (Chapter 6) Interviewing (Chapter 7) Focus Groups (Chapter 8) Portfolios (Chapter 12)	Surveys (Chapter 6) Focus groups (Chapter 8) Portfolios (Chapter 12)
Behavioral	Informal (Chapter 4) Performance (Chapter 11) Portfolios (Chapter 12)	Performance (Chapter 11) Portfolios (Chapter 12)	Portfolios (Chapter 12)
Cognitive	Informal (Chapter 4) CATs (Chapter 5) Knowledge (Chapter 9) Concept maps (Chapter 10) Portfolios (Chapter 12)	Knowledge (Chapter 9) Portfolios (Chapter 12)	Knowledge (Chapter 9) Portfolios (Chapter 12)

Figure 3.1. Quick Guide to Assessment Tools.

Time:

How much time does it take to prepare, administer, and analyze?

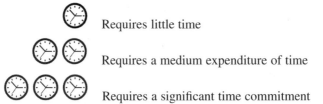

🕐 Requires little time

🕐🕐 Requires a medium expenditure of time

🕐🕐🕐 Requires a significant time commitment

Money:

What level of financial commitment is required to administer the assessment tool?

$ Requires little or no money

$$ Requires some funds for incentives, personnel, or other costs

$$$ Requires significant amount of financial commitment for preparation, administration, or analysis

Level of Assessment:

What setting is the tool most useful for?

 Classroom

Tools with This Icon:

- gather information about learning within one or two classes;
- assess whether students understand concepts presented in a class session;
- can be used for pre- and post-assessment at the beginning and end of a class session or course;
- can assess teaching techniques and analyze their impact on student learning;
- can be used in a 50-minute instruction session or in a semester course.

 Programmatic

Tools with This Icon:

- gather information about a set of classes or courses, within a department or within a library's instructional program;
- can assess how students in a certain major have progressed in terms of information literacy skills from the beginning of a program to the end;
- can be used to gauge how students are receiving information literacy instruction within a department;
- can assess departmental information literacy goals or discipline-specific skills.

 Institutional

Tools with This Icon:

- gather information from across the institution, covering several programs or departments;
- can assess how students' information literacy skills have changed throughout their academic careers;
- can be used to obtain data on how the teaching of information literacy skills is incorporated throughout the curriculum;
- can be used to compare the skill levels of graduating seniors with those at other institutions;
- are effective when doing longitudinal assessment.

Assessment Domain:

What kind of information will the tool tell you about students?

 Affective: Tools that help you assess students' feelings, perceptions, or opinions

 Behavioral: Tools that help you assess how students apply what they have learned and what students can do

 Cognitive: Tools that help you assess what students know

Access to Participants:

How much effort will it take to obtain students as participants?

 Easy: Students are already in your class so you have a captive audience

 Medium: Takes some outreach to contact students; may involve working through faculty to identify and contact a group of students

 Difficult: Involves recruiting students, finding an agreeable time to fit in their schedules, etc.

Level of Faculty Collaboration:

Is the tool one you can implement on your own, or will you need to secure faculty or administrator consent and collaboration?

 Little or no need for faculty collaboration or intervention

 Must get some buy-in and cooperation from faculty

 Requires intense collaboration/partnership with faculty or administration

Outside Expertise:

How much know-how does the tool require?

 No outside expertise needed, should be able to do it on your own

 May need outside help because the tool requires some specialized skills

 Will definitely need outside help or expertise

In addition to the indicator icons, the beginning of the chapters describing the tools includes a brief list of characteristics of the tool. Using the indicators and the characteristics, you can decide at a glance whether a particular tool will work for your assessment situation. Within each chapter, you will see a brief overview of the assessment tool, as well as information on its use. Whenever possible, we have included examples of assessment tools, as well as useful sidebars with additional information. At the end of each chapter, we provide you with a summary of what has been covered and expand on the indicators from the beginning of the chapter. Each chapter includes a list of works cited plus suggestions for additional reading.

Part II

The Tools

4

Informal Assessment Techniques

Indicators:

 Requires little time

 Requires little money

Level of assessment: Classroom

 Domains: Affective, Behavioral, Cognitive

 Easy access to participants

 Little or no need for faculty collaboration

 No outside expertise needed

Key Characteristics:

- Utilizes the natural processes of observation, questioning, and reflection.
- Highly responsive, flexible, and fast.
- Most classroom interactions represent an opportunity for informal assessment.
- Great at generating timely feedback during instruction or just after.
- Can complement other qualitative techniques, such as interviewing and focus groups.
- Requires little advanced planning.
- Helpful in identifying formal assessment needs.
- Relies on inferences, which are susceptible to bias and false assumptions.
- Not a good choice when formal assessment is required.

AN OVERVIEW OF INFORMAL ASSESSMENT

You probably already use informal assessment techniques in your instruction. Examples include asking students questions during or just after a lesson or observing student behaviors during a lesson. Oosterhof writes, "Probably more than 90% of all measures of student performance involve casual observation and questioning…" (2001, p. 191). Though informal assessment has limited value compared with other more standardized methods in producing quality data for written reports, it is the most valuable day-to-day assessment method available to us, and it often supplements other qualitative assessment methods. Most importantly, informal assessment provides us with our most immediate feedback in the classroom and allows us the opportunity to improve our teaching both spontaneously and with reflection.

What exactly do we mean by the phrase "informal assessment?" The phrase appears frequently in the literature of assessment, yet it can have many definitions. Sometimes it refers to any assessment method that is based on nonstandard techniques. In the 1980s, educators began to describe informal assessment as a type of alternative assessment. Alternative assessment seeks to overcome the limitations of pencil and paper testing and provides opportunities for students to directly apply knowledge (Mertler 2003, p. 70).

As we hinted above, it's not so much a question of whether to use informal assessment techniques, but a matter of being aware of the process and making the most of it. Yet, regardless of how good we are in conducting informal assessment, we would never use informal assessment as a stand-alone methodology for formally assessing information literacy. However, informal assessments might fit into your assessment plan as a way of identifying assessment needs. For example, if your informal observations and questions show that students in a class do not seem to know the foundational principles of search strategy, you might consider verifying this observation with a more formal assessment project. The results from both assessments could then be used to design more appropriate instruction for the future.

For our purposes we will define informal assessment as the specific techniques of observing, questioning, and self-reflecting. This chapter will discuss these techniques within the context of the classroom, but feel free to apply informal assessment techniques to any assessment environment where it might be helpful, whether be in the classroom or in a more formal setting, like a focus group session.

Informal Observations

Instructors make informal observations by watching and/or listening to students as they receive instruction or work to accomplish a skill-based activity. Nearly inseparable from the instruction itself, observation is a valuable planning tool that can allow instructors to revise their instruction spontaneously. For example, suppose you have just delivered a lesson on truncating search terms for an online catalog search and have asked students to try truncating a few terms themselves. You will immediately observe students' facial expressions as they address the problem at hand. Confused looks may indicate that you might want to repeat the instructions or be prepared to assist certain students during the exercise.

We should also note that this form of observation is spontaneous and unstructured, differentiating it from other more formal types of observation that involve recording observations and monitoring them via checklists and rating scales.

Informal Questions

Also spontaneous and unstructured, informal questions involve asking students about the lesson being delivered. These questions will usually be posed in direct response to observations. Returning to the above example, the instructor, after observing confused expressions, might ask a few questions such as, "Does anybody have questions?" or "Who wants to try the first one for us at the board?" These questions do not assume that students do not understand. They explore the possibility that they are confused.

Self-Reflection

Working together, observations and questions can be the propelling force of an instructional session, providing feedback that generates questions that generate further feedback that generates further questions, and so on, as the instructor continually reflects upon the goals and objectives of her or his instruction. Reflection or self-reflection, in fact, is the glue that holds this process together, allowing instructors to assess and reassess the effectiveness of their instruction on the spot. In addition, self-reflection can be a great tool for summing up instructional experiences and identifying key questions and concerns.

KEYS TO SUCCESS WITH INFORMAL ASSESSMENT

Although informal assessment does not require a great deal of preparation, some consideration of the process, at least initially, will allow you to be much more effective. Most of you probably already use informal assessment to some degree in your teaching. So consider this a review of the key tips for success with informal observing, questioning, and self-reflection.

Tips for Informal Observations

1. Be Comfortable and Familiar with What is Being Observed

The more comfortable and knowledgeable you are with your lesson plan and classroom setting, the better an observer you will be. This is really common sense. Compare your first time doing a task with your later attempts and almost always your later experiences will be more successful. Teaching experience plays an important role in achieving an optimum comfort level. The more interactions you have with students regarding the content of your lesson, the more effective you will become as an observer. Without a high level of familiarity with the content of your lesson, you are less likely to <u>know</u> what you should and should not be looking for with your observations.

2. Identify What You Will Observe

We can only observe a small portion of behaviors that are potentially observable, so it is crucial that we focus our observations on those behaviors that are the most telling and significant. Your instructional goals will provide the basis for what you should be observing, and if you have written thorough learning outcomes, this will make the process much easier, as you will already have identified measurable and observable behaviors. If not, your challenge will be to translate your instructional goals into observable behaviors. Using our earlier example in which students were taught truncation in a library catalog, the instructor might include among the behaviors to observe students' ability to identify situations in which it is appropriate to use truncation or students' ability to correctly truncate search terms according to the library catalog's rules.

3. Limit How Much You Will Observe

This follows from our previous point. We are limited in the number of behaviors we can observe. Though you may have three instructional goals with several related objectives for your lesson, you will not be able to focus on observing all of these. It is best to focus on only one or two skills or outcomes, especially if you are inexperienced. The more experience you gain, the more you will be able to observe. So start small to position yourself for success.

4. Record Key Observations in Key Situations

Sometimes recording informal observations is unnecessary and impractical. It may be unnecessary because observations provide instantaneous feedback that is often best used immediately to adjust what's going on in the classroom; impractical because recording can take too long. However, in some cases, you may want to record your significant observations. This may be helpful when you are working with several classes or when you and your colleagues are teaching the same content to different classes. This can be done informally as well. Simply jot your notes on a pad of paper. Try to write down a key phrase or a reminder of what your observation was.

Tips for Informal Questioning

I. Base Your Questions on Your Instructional Goals

Again, your instructional goals provide a good starting point for informal questions. Before your first instructional session, spend some time reviewing your goals and brainstorming about potential questions. This may seem to contradict the spontaneous nature of informal questioning, but remember, we said informal assessment techniques require little planning, not zero planning.

Ask yourself whether simply asking students to recall a fact or piece of knowledge (for example, what is an abstract?) assesses your goal or whether a deeper line of questioning is required. Goals that involve processes and/or complex evaluation may require a series of questions to fully assess.

Also, remind yourself that this is a process: observations, questions, and self-reflection. Your observations will generate additional questions. You will listen and observe students as they answer questions. You will reflect on their behaviors and answers, and you will ask more questions and make additional observations.

2. Communicate Effectively

In addition to asking the right questions, you will want to strive to be an effective communicator. The way in which you ask the questions can affect the responses you get. Here are some key considerations for communicating your questions effectively:

• **Be Clear and Concise:** This is an area where a little preparation can go a long way. Take time before a session to run through your potential questions. You want students to understand clearly what you are asking. Even though students will have an opportunity to ask for clarification, it is best to work toward clarity in advance of informally questioning students. Also, because you will be asking additional questions orally, take time to phrase your questions in your mind before putting them to students.

- **Give Students Sufficient Time to Respond:** This may seem like common sense, but it is one of the most common errors made by instructors. While questions that ask students to recall information often draw quick responses, complex questions will require extra time. As instructors, we often feel uncomfortable with prolonged silence and rush to fill the void by answering our own questions. However, next time, try waiting it out. Eventually someone will volunteer, even if it is under his or her breath.
- **Avoid Making Students Uncomfortable:** Informal questions usually take place in group settings, meaning that students will be asked to answer in the presence of their peers. This in itself may embarrass and make students uncomfortable. So take steps to avoid any further ratcheting up of the stress in the classroom. You can control this to a great extent by accepting and reacting positively to student responses. Do not dwell on incorrect answers. Turn things in a positive light and move on.

Tips for Instructor Self-Reflection

Instructor self-reflection plays two important roles as an informal assessment technique. First, it helps connect our observations and questions, allowing us to assess and reassess the effectiveness of our instruction on the spot. Second, it can serve as a way to wrap-up or process an instructional experience, drawing upon observations and student responses, raising important questions and findings. While the first use of self-reflection is integrated into the process of observing and questioning, which we have already discussed, the second use can be discussed as a separate process. Here are a few tips for using self-reflection to process an instruction session.

1. Make Time for Self-Reflection

Most self-reflection comes naturally, but you need to make time to sit down after your instruction session has concluded to hold a self-debriefing or a self-reflection session. This can last anywhere from 5 to 20 minutes and consists of reviewing your instruction session and reflecting on key observations and student responses. However it will not happen if you do not allow time for it. So include it in your instructional planning process to make sure it happens.

2. Consider Creating an Informal Assessment Record

An informal assessment record, sometimes called an anecdotal record, is a narrative description of observations and student responses with instructor reflection and interpretation included. Creating informal assessment records by way of a form can streamline the process of reflecting on an instruction session, making it easier for you to focus on the key elements of your experience. You can include whatever fields you think necessary, but in general consider including: title of session, date of session, a description of goals and objectives, a summary of key observations and student responses, your thoughts and reactions to these observations and responses and space to list any resulting questions, and conclusions or actions that you identify. Figure 4.1 illustrates a sample informal assessment form.

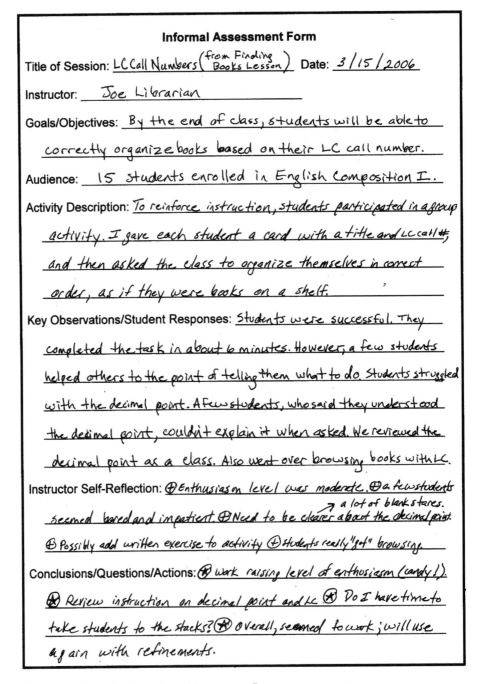

Informal Assessment Form

Title of Session: LC Call Numbers (from Finding Books Lesson)   Date: 3/15/2006

Instructor: Joe Librarian

Goals/Objectives: By the end of class, students will be able to correctly organize books based on their LC call number.

Audience: 15 students enrolled in English Composition I.

Activity Description: To reinforce instruction, students participated in a group activity. I gave each student a card with a title and LC call #, and then asked the class to organize themselves in correct order, as if they were books on a shelf.

Key Observations/Student Responses: Students were successful. They completed the task in about 6 minutes. However, a few students helped others to the point of telling them what to do. Students struggled with the decimal point. A few students, who said they understood the decimal point, couldn't explain it when asked. We reviewed the decimal point as a class. Also went over browsing books with LC.

Instructor Self-Reflection: ⊕ Enthusiasm level was moderate. ⊕ a few students seemed bored and impatient. → a lot of blank stares. ⊖ Need to be clearer about the decimal point. ⊕ Possibly add written exercise to activity ⊕ Students really "got" browsing.

Conclusions/Questions/Actions: ✱ work raising level of enthusiasm (candy!). ✱ Review instruction on decimal point and LC ✱ Do I have time to take students to the stacks? ✱ Overall, seemed to work; will use again with refinements.

Figure 4.1. Example of an Informal Assessment Form.

3. Review Observations and Responses in Context of Your Lesson Plan

This simply means to reflect on key observations and student responses as they relate to the goals and objectives of your lesson. In the sample informal assessment record illustrated in Figure 4.1, the objective of a lesson on Library of Congress call numbers is for students to be able to order books correctly by call number. A group activity directly following library instruction provided the opportunity for students to accomplish this. It follows then that the instructor focused his observations and questions on this activity. He noted student nonverbal and verbal behaviors as they related to accomplishing the lesson's objective. After the session, when the instructor reflected and completed his informal assessment record, he returned to these observed behaviors and responses and first, recorded them and second, reacted to and interpreted them. He then noted any conclusions, questions, or comments that arose out of his reflection. This provided valuable information that could be incorporated into future instruction sessions.

USING THE DATA FROM INFORMAL ASSESSMENT

We have already talked at length about the how the data from informal assessment techniques can be used. Largely, data from informal assessments are reflected upon and fed back into the assessment/instructional process. These reflections often lead to improved or revised classroom techniques and strategies. They may also point to the need for further assessment using more formal or standardized methods. The best way to use the data from informal assessment is to strive to integrate it into your day-to-day instruction, thereby making informal assessment techniques a regular part of your teaching process.

IS INFORMAL ASSESSMENT RIGHT FOR YOU?

Review the following factors when considering informal assessment:

 Time

Informal assessment is time friendly. It requires little preplanning and takes place during class time. However, if you have not consciously worked on informal assessment during your instruction, some initial planning and preparation time can help you master the process. Later, when informal assessment has become part of your teaching process, you will be able to take full advantage of the method's time efficiencies.

 Money

Informal assessment is extremely cheap. The only real cost is the intellectual effort required of you to use it effectively.

 Level of Assessment

Informal assessment techniques are used predominantly in classroom settings. The subjective nature of this method and the fact that it might be used differently in three separate classes teaching the same lesson make informal assessment a poor choice for program level assessment, unless its techniques are used simply to supplement other methods.

Assessment Domains

Informal assessment techniques reach across learning domains, allowing instructors to informally assess student knowledge, feelings, and behaviors, but as stressed earlier, it does not produce formal, shareable results. Informal assessment at its most informal is a way of evaluating "how things are going" during a lesson, and at its most formal it can point out needs for future assessments and give you a strong sense of the learning culture of your students.

 Access to Participants

Informal assessment techniques require a high degree of accessibility. If you are teaching a lesson, you have the opportunity to use informal assessment. However, as librarians, who usually are not the lead instructors for courses, we need opportunities for classroom interactions (see Level of Faculty Collaboration below).

 Level of Faculty Collaboration

Faculty collaboration is necessary in that as librarians we usually need to collaborate with faculty to have instructional opportunities. However, beyond this initial collaboration, we could pursue informal assessments free of further in-depth faculty–librarian consultation. We should be open to sharing our informal assessment results with faculty, as our results can help a faculty member gain a better understand the class's level of learning and the role your instruction plays in developing and supporting it.

 Outside Expertise

Informal assessment does not require the aid of outside experts. It should be noted, however, that the more skill and expertise you develop in using informal assessments, the more rewarding you will find the process and its results.

WORKS CITED AND FURTHER READING

Airasian, P. W. (2000). *Assessment in the classroom: A concise approach* (2nd ed.). Boston: McGraw-Hill.

Mertler, C. A. (2003). *Classroom assessment: A practical guide for educators*. Los Angeles, CA: Pyrczak Publishing.

Oosterhof, A. (2001). *Classroom applications of educational measurement*. Upper Saddle River, NJ: Merrill.

Rinvolucri, M. (2003). How I pay attention in class. *Essential Teacher, 1*(1), 51–53.

Taylor, G. R. (2003). *Informal classroom assessment strategies for teachers*. Lanham, MD: Scarecrow Press.

5

Classroom Assessment Techniques

Indicators:

 Requires little time

 Requires little money

 Level of assessment: Classroom

 Domain: Affective, Cognitive

Easy access to participants

 Little or no need for faculty collaboration

 No outside expertise needed

Key Characteristics:

- Used in classroom settings or as follow-up to instruction session.
- Practical and action-oriented.
- Provides immediate feedback on students' perceptions and knowledge.
- Can be tailored to a specific concept or unit.
- Formative in nature.
- Provides a snapshot of comprehension. However, will not tell you how well students are integrating information literacy into their work.
- Should be used to initiate changes in instruction to enhance student learning.

AN OVERVIEW OF CLASSROOM ASSESSMENT TECHNIQUES

Developed by Tom Angelo and Patricia Cross in the late 1980s, classroom assessment techniques (CATs) are designed for easy inclusion in a class session and provide an excellent snapshot of student learning at a particular point in time. This kind of assessment is formative in that you are assessing while students are in the process of learning. CATs can be used to discover whether students understand a particular concept, as well as to determine what questions students still have about the material.

The overlying principle is simple: you first ask your students to do a brief reflection related to the instruction that has been provided in class. For example, you might have students write down one new piece of information that they didn't know about the research process prior to the instruction session, or have them list one concept that still confuses them. You then collect the responses and use the information to enhance your instruction and to provide students with feedback that will improve their learning.

Classroom assessment techniques help you assess whether students are grasping information literacy skills at the point of instruction. According to Cross and Angelo (1988, p. 12), CATs answer the following questions:

- How many students are learning the content?
- Which elements of the course content are students learning?
- What specifically should you change about your teaching to promote optimal learning?

Assessment is a circular rather than a linear process. Good assessment leads to improved teaching and then reassessment of that teaching. In Figure 5.1, Angelo and Cross describe ten major steps that are part of the classroom assessment process.

PREPARATION

Classroom assessment is most effective when it is linked to teaching goals and learning objectives. In the late 1980s, Angelo and Cross developed a *Teaching Goals Inventory* to help instructors identify the primary goals and priorities for courses they teach. The *Teaching Goals Inventory* is currently hosted by the University of Iowa at www.uiowa.edu/~centeach/tgi/index.html. The more-than-50 items that make up the goals inventory are general in nature and do not focus on specific content. To use the inventory, first choose a course that you teach. Then rank each of your goals for that course on a five-part scale from Not Applicable to Essential. The next step is to pull out the goals that rank high on the scale and build a lesson plan around those goals. A CAT that matches the teaching goals can then be selected.

For example, if one of your essential goals in teaching a class on the use of the Web is that students will be able to distinguish between fact and opinion, then your instruction should help students understand how to look for bias in a Web site. The classroom assessment should then provide an opportunity for students to demonstrate whether they have grasped this "essential" concept. You could use a CAT that requires students to write down three clues that could be used in determining whether a Web site deals in facts or opinions. See Figure 5.2 for more details on the inventory.

Angelo and Cross strongly recommend (1993) that you first undertake classroom assessment in a course or class in which you believe your instructional goals are actually being met. This will provide you with incentive to improve upon your instruction

STEP 1: Choose one course that you currently teach and that you have taught before. Choose a class that is going well.

STEP 2: Identify a single teaching and learning goal and then develop an assessable question.

STEP 3: Choose an appropriate assessment technique based on your question and the time you have to administer and evaluate results.

STEP 4: Be prepared to adequately and thoroughly cover the material you are going to assess. Check your lesson plan against the assessment you expect students to do.

STEP 5: Administer the technique in the class, making sure to explain it carefully. If administering for the first time, allow a little more time than you think it will take.

STEP 6: Analyze student feedback, making sure to look at the whole range of responses. Don't focus your energy on 1 or 2 negative responses.

STEP 7: Spend some time figuring out why you received the responses you did. Did you fail to cover the material adequately? Was the assessment tool chosen not the "correct" one? Did your class preparation pay off?

STEP 8: Do something with the results. Provide students with feedback. If the results were positive, pat yourself on the back, and then look for ways you can make your instruction even better.

STEP 9: Reflect on the use and value of classroom assessment. What did you learn from the experience? What can you share with your colleagues?

STEP 10: Plan future assessment that might build on or complement the classroom assessment you have done.

Figure 5.1. Ten Major Steps to Classroom Assessment.

Source: Angelo, T. A. and Cross, P. (1993). *Classroom assessment techniques: A handbook for college teachers* (2nd ed.). San Francisco: Jossey-Bass Publishers.

rather than just using a CAT to confirm that students are not "getting it." Also, focus on one course at a time. For example, if your typical semester instruction load consists of multiple sessions of an English composition class, four sections of an introductory sociology class, and two sections of a psychology research methods course, choose one of those disciplines to assess at a time. This will allow you enough time to actually complete the cycle from establishing objectives through to incorporating feedback into your instruction.

The nature of classroom assessment dictates that you limit the number of questions you ask in your assessment. This is not a survey or a test. Students should not find this to be an onerous task and, realistically, you may be able to devote only so much of your limited class time to assessment.

Typically CATs are used at the end of a class session, but they can be introduced at any point during the instruction. In fact, if the class seems to be fading a bit, taking a couple minutes to introduce a CAT can perk up the energy level. It also makes students aware that you value their opinion (if you are asking about perceptions) or that you do expect them to pay attention to content (if you are asking them to demonstrate knowledge).

Originally developed by Angelo and Cross (1993), the *Teaching Goals Inventory* is currently hosted by the University of Iowa at www.uiowa.edu/~centeach/tgi/index.html.

When taking the *Teaching Goals Inventory* first choose one course that you are currently teaching. Then scan through the items to get a sense of the overall content. This inventory is not specific to information literacy skills; it is intended to cover concepts that might be taught in a variety of instructional settings.

Goals that you will be asked to rank include the following:

- Develop problem solving skills
- Develop ability to distinguish between fact and opinion
- Improve reading skills
- Learn to evaluate methods and materials in this subject
- Improve ability to work productively with others

Goals are ranked according to the following scale:

1. Not applicable	A goal you never try to achieve.
2. Unimportant	A goal you rarely try to achieve.
3. Important	A goal you sometimes try to achieve.
4. Very important	A goal you often try to achieve.
5. Essential	A goal you always/nearly always try to achieve.

Figure 5.2. Sample Questions from the *Teaching Goals Inventory*.

As you prepare for classroom assessment, it is helpful to begin by answering the following two questions by completing the corresponding statements.

- What is it that you want to know about your students' learning? Complete this statement: "I want to know whether my students . . . ."
- What do you think the assessment will accomplish? Complete this statement: "Ideally, the information I collect will tell me . . . ." (Searle, 1999, p. 28)

Answering these questions will provide you with a good foundation from which to choose the assessment technique that will provide you with the best answers to your questions.

EXAMPLES OF CLASSROOM ASSESSMENT TECHNIQUES

Classroom assessment techniques come in all sizes and shapes. As mentioned previously, some CATs work very effectively within the time constraints under which librarians do instruction. Four of those CATs (*Minute Paper/Muddiest Point, One Sentence Summary, Defining Features Matrix*, and *Directed Paraphrasing*) are described here and if you are new to classroom assessment, you might want to start with one of them. Other CATs were developed with classroom faculty in mind. These work best when you are doing instruction over the course of several sessions or when you are teaching a course. You will want to consult Angelo and Cross's *Classroom Assessment Techniques: A Handbook for College Teachers* for additional CATs and select those that best fit your assessment needs.

Minute Paper/Muddiest Point

The Minute Paper (often paired with the Muddiest Point) provides immediate feedback as to a student's overall sense of her or his own learning. It is a reflective exercise and actually includes two questions. Students are first asked to describe the most important thing that they learned in class (or some variation of this question, such as "What was one new thing that you learned today?").

In an instruction session in which you focus on database searching, you might expect responses like:

- *That you can use the asterisk (*) at the end of words to get more results.*
- *I learned how to narrow my searches when I get too many results.*
- *I learned how to tell whether an article is from a scholarly journal.*
- *That you can e-mail articles to yourself.*

The answers may not always please you, especially if you spent a significant amount of time on one concept and no students mention it in their lists of things they have learned, but the answers are valid for those students and need to be taken at face value. If their responses reflect something that you did teach them, even if it was not the main focus of your instruction, then you do have evidence that some learning was taking place.

Be prepared, however, for responses such as: "I didn't learn anything new" or "I learned that the librarian gives out candy." Not all students will value this assessment tool as much as you do!

In the second part of the Minute Paper (known as the Muddiest Point), students are asked to write down a question they still have about the material. You might ask "What questions do you still have about what was covered in class today?" or "List something that you wish the instructor had spent more time explaining."

In a typical "one shot" library instruction session in which you cover a lot of material, you might expect responses like:

- *How do I actually find a book on the shelf in the library?*
- *How do I get an article if it is not available online?*
- *How do I tell which database to use for my topic?*
- *I still don't understand how to tell if a Web site is good.*

You will also get responses such as, "Nothing was confusing. I understand everything." Even if you suspect this might not be true, you must again take the response at face value. This is the student's assessment of his or her own learning.

Administering the Minute Paper

The Minute Paper and the Muddiest Point can be administered alone or together as a two-question assessment. In either case, begin by asking students to get out a piece of paper or distribute index cards or blank pieces of paper. Write the question that you want students to answer on the white board, chalkboard, or overhead. It is helpful to students if the question appears in writing somewhere since attention spans differ and, for some students, seeing the question in writing will help them process their thoughts. You can also distribute a card or paper with the question already written on it.

Inform the students that they have two or three minutes to respond to the question. If it is important to you that students write in complete sentences, make that expectation clear at the beginning, though generally you will want students to focus on the content, not the grammar or format. Stick to the time period. The idea is for students to give you their immediate impressions and not try to second guess what you want. Remember also that if you are doing the assessment at the end of the class, students will be anxious to finish the task and leave the classroom. (Don't take this personally. It happens to even the most dynamic teacher!) Allow the students to answer anonymously, although you can offer them the option of adding their names and e-mail addresses if they want you to answer their questions directly.

One Sentence Summary

In this CAT, students are asked to summarize their knowledge of a particular concept that has been covered in class in <u>one sentence</u>. As conceived by Angelo and Cross (1993, p. 183), the One Sentence Summary should answer the questions, "Who does what to whom, when, where, how, and why?" Keep in mind, however, that you have flexibility in how you administer this CAT and whether you want to insist that all seven questions be addressed in the one sentence.

In order to make students feel that this is a worthwhile exercise, choose a concept that is important to information literacy or one that you spent a lot of time covering in class. The point of this assessment is not to "trip students up," but rather to assess whether students have internalized the information you want them to learn.

If you intend to use the One Sentence Summary, it is important for you to compile a list of possible answers ahead of time. This will assist you in determining the difficulty level of the question and provide you with your own checklist of acceptable answers. See Figure 5.3 for an example using this technique.

It may be very difficult for some students to grasp this assessment technique and not all concepts lend themselves to being easily summarized in one sentence. You may end up getting responses that do not answer all of the questions such as this one: *If the word "and" is put between two different words in an online catalog search, I will get fewer book titles.*

Remember that the actual wording is less important than assessing whether students understand the logic of using Boolean connectors. In this example, the response does reflect an understanding of narrowing results. In addition to writing a sentence, you could also ask students to provide you with an example of how they would use the Boolean operator "and" in a search statement.

If time allows, you can have students work cooperatively by asking them to write their answers individually and then compare notes with a few other students. Have the group write one response incorporating all group members' ideas on a large sheet of paper. These can be posted at the front of the class and the results can be compared between groups. Think about using this approach as a way of introducing active learning into your classroom, rather than as an extraneous add-on to your instruction. You will be getting feedback about their learning and they will be reinforcing the concepts. See Figure 5.4 for tips on facilitating group work.

The One Sentence Summary is a technique that can be used multiple times throughout the semester. The more opportunities that students have to practice the technique, the easier it will be for them to answer the questions and the less time will be required for the assessment.

Ask the students to explain in their own words (and in one grammatically correct sentence) the purpose of using the Boolean operator "AND" when searching in an online catalog for books on a specific topic.

To guide students through the process, provide them with a list of the questions you want answered and encourage them to try to answer as many as possible for the topic they are summarizing. For this Boolean operator example, a completed list might look like this:

WHO or WHAT?	The Boolean operator "AND"
DOES WHAT?	limits or narrows
TO WHAT OR WHOM?	search results
WHEN?	in a keyword search
WHERE?	in the online catalog
HOW?	by joining two different concepts
WHY?	in order to provide a list of books that are most appropriate for my topic.

The resulting One Sentence Summary would then read like this:

The Boolean operator "AND" limits or narrows search results in a keyword search in the online catalog by joining two different concepts in order to provide a list of books that are most appropriate for my topic.

Figure 5.3. Example of a One Sentence Summary Assessment.

If you are doing even the smallest amount of group work during an instruction session, establishing the partnerships or groups at the beginning of the class can save time later. If you have a class of 25 or 30, place one square of colored paper on each desk, table, or chair where the students will be sitting, with each color representing a group. This avoids confusion when there are uneven numbers of students and reduces the chaos of having students choose their own groups. Later, you can just tell students to group themselves by the color of the paper in front of them.

If you are going to have students work with a partner, then orchestrate the selection process at the beginning of the class, so that if you tell the students to "consult with their partner" they will know with whom they should be talking.

Large lecture halls are more problematic. Check out natural breaks in the seating arrangement for clues as to how you can assign groups. You can give "Bill" who is sitting in the last row of the lecture hall a slip of blue paper and then give another slip of blue paper to "Janet" who is sitting two rows in front of Bill. Tell students that anyone sitting between Bill and Janet is in the blue group. Repeat this process with the rest of the class. Much of the extra time required to do group projects comes from the confusion in establishing the groups in the first place. A little preparation on your part will help reduce that confusion and establish a group identity among the students.

Figure 5.4. Facilitating Group Work.

Defining Features Matrix

This tool can be used in situations when you want students to demonstrate that they understand the differences or similarities between concepts, resources, or methodologies. Choose two or three concepts that you cover in class and that students often get mixed up (for example, the differences between scholarly and popular articles). Then draw up a list of characteristics or features of each concept (for example, a scholarly article has an extended list of references at the end of the article). From that complete list, choose 8 to 12 features that you feel students should easily be able to identify (peer-reviewed, written for a general audience, include color photos or ads, etc.).

Then create a matrix with the features down the left side and the concepts or resources across the top. Figure 5.5 provides an example of a matrix comparing the features of an online catalog and a database. Test out the matrix to make sure that the answers are clear—this is not the place for subtleties or nuances. Make copies of the matrix and distribute to the students after your instruction. If you wish to assess student perceptions and knowledge before and after your instruction, conduct this assessment both at the beginning and at the end of the class.

To complete the matrix, students should enter a plus sign (+) or the word "yes" in the column if the concept has one of the features and a negative sign (−) or the word "no" if it does not have that feature. Inform students that some concepts may be positive for both features.

The defined matrix is easy to score (you just need to compare your matrix to the completed student matrix), and can help you to quickly gauge whether students can distinguish between concepts or resources. Students can be asked to complete the matrix during class so that you can provide them with immediate feedback, or at the beginning of a class so that you can gauge the level of student knowledge before you begin instruction.

The creation of the matrix may take a bit more time than the scoring (especially if you are trying to help students understand more abstract concepts). As you probably cover similar topics in many different instruction sessions (even across disciplines), you will be able to use the matrix more than once, which makes the effort worthwhile.

Directed Paraphrasing

This assessment technique involves asking students to explain the content of what has been covered in a particular class to a specific audience. It provides a method for students to explain the content of what they have learned in more detail than the One Sentence Summary. Providing a context for the assignment requires students to do more than just parrot back the information and makes the assessment seem more practical to them. Figure 5.6 explains this technique more fully through an example.

PRE-ASSESSMENT USING CATs

CATs can be used prior to the beginning of a class for a quick assessment of knowledge and attitudes. You can conduct the assessment at the beginning of your instructional session, or you might ask the faculty member to take a few minutes from her or his own class time to administer your pre-assessment and then pass the information on to you in advance. Remember that we are referring to classroom assessment here and not the administration of long questionnaires or surveys, which are covered in Chapter 6.

	Online Catalog	Research Database
Use to identify which books are owned by the library.	+	−
Searches provide citations to journal and magazine articles.	−	+
Allows use of Boolean connectors in keyword searches.	+	+
Allows you to email articles to yourself.	−	+
Provides call number to help you locate item on library shelf.	+	−
Allows you to view a search history.	+	+
Often provides table of contents for book.	+	−
Search result provides you with the information you will need for your citations.	+	+
Usually provides an abstract of an article.	−	+
Find It feature links to information about availability.	−	+
Searches adjacent words as a phrase.	+	+

Figure 5.5. Example of Defining Features Matrix.

After teaching a session on Web evaluation, you provide students with this scenario:

> *You are asked to do a presentation to fourth grade students on how to select appropriate Web sites for a project they are doing on dinosaurs. In language that a fourth grader would understand, list three criteria they should use to evaluate Web sites.*

Keep in mind that this technique will require more time than the previous two classroom assessment techniques and might be assigned as "homework" to be turned in at the next class (if you are teaching a semester course), or to the faculty member for whom you are doing the instruction. The danger of lengthier classroom assessment is that students will want to know whether the exercise "counts." Being able to have a faculty member reinforce the importance of the exercise will help buy-in considerably.

Figure 5.6. Example of Directed Paraphrasing.

Pre-assessment in this context is used to gain a better sense of student knowledge of one or two specific concepts, allowing you to get a snapshot of the class you will be teaching and prepare accordingly. If appropriate, you can have students complete a version of the pre-assessment at the end of the instruction session in order to measure the learning that took place. See Figure 5.7 for an example.

You could also do a pre-assessment of students' expectations by asking students what questions they would most like to have answered during the instruction session. It is recommended that you have students do this in writing either in their "regular" class or while they are getting settled in your instruction session. We know from experience that

You are teaching an upper-level course in *Human Development and Aging* and want to gauge students' familiarity with the databases you plan to cover in your session.

While students are getting settled, give them three slips of paper with a different database listed at the top of each slip, for example, *Academic Search Premier*, *PsycINFO*, *Ageline*.

Ask the students to write the number 1, 2, or 3 on each piece of paper to reflect their prior knowledge of the resource: 1 = never used; 2 = used once or twice; 3 = used frequently. Collect the cards and sort them out in the front of the class or ask for a volunteer to help you sort them while you get settled with your introductions. Although you will inevitably have a range of responses, this exercise provides you with a better sense of which resources you can review only and which you need to spend more time on.

An alternative method of gathering this information, one that can help students get more involved, is to use a white board or large flip chart pads. Give students three sets of different colors of stickers (or sticky notes): red for never used, blue for used once or twice, and green for used frequently. Hang three different flip chart sheets on the wall (one for each database) and have students place the appropriate colored stickers on the sheets. You can then see at a glance how students rate their expertise. One possible downside to this approach is that a student might be intimidated if he or she sees that a large number of students in the class indicating a good working knowledge of a resource, and that student is a novice. Reassure students that it is okay to admit that they don't have extensive experience with the databases.

You could easily follow-up this assessment later in the semester by asking students to repeat the exercise. The results would not tell you about how the student uses the database or evaluates the information retrieved, but it would provide an indication of whether instruction on additional resources makes a difference in students' choice of research tools.

Figure 5.7. Example of Conducting a Pre-Assessment.

asking students to verbally articulate their questions usually results in blank stares or minimal participation at best.

If you have asked for student input, then make sure you address at least a few of their questions during your class. At the end of the instruction, ask students what questions they still have by using the Muddiest Point. This will tell you immediately whether your instruction was effective and provides you with pre- and post-instruction data.

CLASSROOM RESPONSE SYSTEMS

Although the CATs described so far in this chapter use traditional paper and pen methods for feedback, there is another option that involves more sophisticated technology. Classroom response systems, also known as audience response systems or personal response systems, consist of a transmitter used by students to submit responses, a receiver attached to the instructor's computer that captures the responses, and software that interprets and displays the results. The system can be set up using either infrared, radio frequency, or wireless transmission. The setup depends on the specific system that is used.

The system allows you to create questions (usually true/false or multiple-choice) that can be displayed through a PowerPoint-type interface. Students are asked to respond to each question by using their transmitters (sometimes called clickers). A clicker typically looks like a remote control, consisting of a keypad with numbers or letters that are used for the responses. After everyone has answered, the results are aggregated by the software program and can be displayed to the class. A typical display, using bar graphs or percentage reporting, might show that 70% of students chose option A, 15% chose option B, 5% chose option C, and so on.

This visual display provides a way for an individual student to see if he or she has answered correctly without having to raise a hand or be graded. Although it might be personally embarrassing for the student who realizes he or she is the only one who gave an incorrect answer, neither individual names nor clicker numbers are displayed, thus ensuring anonymity. Instructors do have options for using the response systems to track individual students, but in the classroom assessment context this is not typically done.

The classroom response system can be used off and on to pose questions throughout your instruction session. The immediate assessment that the system provides can indicate whether you need to spend more time on a concept or whether you can move on with some level of confidence that students "get it." This type of assessment is usually more knowledge-based than affective-based. The wording of the assessment questions becomes more critical because you want to make sure the questions you write will accurately assess the content you are teaching. See the section on "Preparing Good Objective Items" in Chapter 9 for guidance.

Check with educational technology personnel at your institution to see if classroom response systems are already in use on your campus. You may be able to see how they are used and to discover how the units are purchased. Sometimes students are expected to purchase clickers as a requirement for a course; sometimes systems are purchased by departments and are attached to a classroom. You could also investigate whether there are portable units on your campus that are available for you to check out. If you want to purchase a system for your library expect to spend about $2,500 for one receiver and 30 clickers. Software is incorporated into the price and usually updates are free over the life of the equipment. Exact costs and conditions vary by manufacturer.

Students seem genuinely engaged with this method of assessment because it provides immediate feedback. They want to find out whether they answered a question correctly and how they fared compared to the rest of the class. It is similar to watching a game show on TV—you answer the question in your living room and then get verification on the TV screen. Classroom response systems are also used at many colleges and universities in large lecture classes. They provide an opportunity for student interaction that is often otherwise more difficult in those settings. In any setting, the goal of using classroom response systems is the same as that of CATs in general—to assess student learning and to incorporate that assessment back into the learning cycle to improve that learning.

USING THE RESULTS

During the introductory phase of your classroom instruction, it is useful to convey to students that their learning is important to you and that you will be assessing that learning at some point during the class. This demonstrates to students that you take the instruction seriously and that you expect them to do so as well. It also helps them understand that you value their learning.

After administering the CAT, read through the collected responses while the instruction session is still fresh in your mind. This provides an immediate sense of students' learning. Then, when you have more time, sort responses to see if there are patterns. What was it about your instruction that "stuck" with students? What do they still find confusing and why? You will undoubtedly be able to see overall patterns, even though there will always be a few unique responses. Acknowledge, but do not dwell on, negative responses.

Remember that classroom assessment is used to improve student learning and, therefore, feedback is critical. The responsibility is in your hands to do something with the information you have collected. The amount of time that you will need to spend on follow-up will depend on the level of response you plan to provide to students. The feedback does not take the form of a grade, but rather involves providing students with additional information based on the data you have collected from them.

For example, if you asked students to reflect on the Muddiest Point in your instruction session and there is an overwhelming consensus that one particular area of instruction is problematic, it is imperative that you follow-up in some way so as to improve students' understanding of this concept. The time required for this feedback will depend on the responses, the number of students in the class, and the level of follow-up you choose to do. Though it may take you only a minute to look at each response, you may end up spending one or two hours on providing feedback.

If you are teaching a semester course or will see students in a subsequent session, you can reintroduce the material (perhaps using a different teaching technique). If you will not have an opportunity to physically meet with the students, summarize the key points in the form of a handout or Web page and pass the information on to the faculty member for distribution.

If you are doing instruction for a faculty member with whom you have a good working relationship, you can share the results of the assessment with him or her and ask for 10 minutes follow-up in the class to answer outstanding questions. If you teach the same content in multiple sections of a course, you may want to get feedback on different concepts in different classes and then combine the feedback to inform your teaching. In all cases, you should use the assessment information as you develop lesson plans for subsequent instruction sessions covering the same material. The next group of students will benefit from the assessment you have already done. The overall goal is to use assessment results to initiate changes that will enhance student learning.

ARE CLASSROOM ASSESSMENT TECHNIQUES RIGHT FOR YOU?

Review the following factors when considering CATs:

 Time

Classroom assessment techniques are not time intensive. Many require only a few minutes of class time to administer, although there are others that might require 10 minutes or more. There are many CATs to choose from and you can select those that best fit into the time you have available. Keep in mind that in addition to the time you need to administer the CATs, you will need to spend time analyzing the data, providing feedback to students, and incorporating changes into your instruction. The time required for this component may range from one hour to five or six hours per class depending on your situation.

 Money

There is little or no cost involved with CATs unless you buy a classroom response system.

 Level of Assessment

It is fairly obvious that CATs should be used when you want to do assessment at the classroom or course level.

 Assessment Domains

Generally you will use CATs to assess students' comprehension of concepts or to get a snapshot of what they have learned in a limited context. Although the emphasis is primarily on assessing their knowledge (cognitive domain), CATs also provide an opportunity to better understand how your teaching has affected students' perceptions of the material (affective domain). Asking a student what he or she learned during class is as much about the facts as it is about what stuck with them. In other words, did your instruction make a difference?

 Access to Participants

You need to have access to students when they are in your instructional session.

 Level of Faculty Collaboration

Because you have control over the administration of CATs and the analysis of the data, the required level of faculty collaboration is low. As mentioned earlier in this chapter, you may want to work with faculty to do some pre-assessment before your instruction or ask classroom faculty to administer a CAT during the first class meeting immediately following your instruction. You may also ask the faculty member to distribute follow-up material that you prepare based on CAT results.

 Outside Expertise

You have all the knowledge and experience needed to administer CATs. First try those with which you feel most comfortable or which require the least amount of preparation (like the One Minute Paper). Once you are comfortable with the approach, move on to other CATs.

WORKS CITED AND FURTHER READING

Angelo, T. A. (1998). *Classroom assessment and research: An update on uses, approaches, and research findings*. San Francisco, CA: Jossey-Bass Publishers.

Angelo, T. A. and Cross, P. (1993). *Classroom assessment techniques: A handbook for college teachers* (2nd ed.). San Francisco, CA: Jossey-Bass Publishers.

Bruff, D. (2007). *Classroom response systems*. Retrieved April 16, 2007 www.vanderbilt.edu/cft/resources/teaching_resources/technology/crs.htm.

Cross, P. and Angelo, T. A. (1988). *Classroom assessment techniques: A handbook for faculty*. Ann Arbor, MI: National Center for Research to Improve Postsecondary Teaching and Learning.

Searle, B. (1999). *Classroom assessment: A manual for faculty developers*. Davenport, IA: National Council for Staff, Program, and Organizational Development.

Stewart, S. L. (1999). Assessment for library instruction: The Cross/Angelo model. *Research Strategies, 16*(3), 165–174.

6

Surveys

Indicators:

 Requires a medium amount of time

 Requires some funds

 Level of assessment: Classroom, Programmatic, Institutional

 Domain: Affective

 Access to participants: Requires medium level of effort; may need collaboration from faculty or other units on campus

 Faculty collaboration not required but helpful and recommended

 Outside expertise may be helpful if in-house skill and experience are not available

Key Characteristics:

- May be used for evaluating the effectiveness of a program or gathering information for further research.
- Usually an efficient and cost-effective way to gather input from many people.
- Can apply results from a representative sample to a larger group.
- May be done on paper or online through e-mail or a Web page.
- Is a familiar format that respondents can complete quickly.
- May incur costs for distribution of survey or incentives for respondents.

- Requires careful planning and organization.
- Offers no opportunity to clarify responses or probe for more information.
- Usually responses have little depth or detail.

AN OVERVIEW OF SURVEYS

Surveys allow us to gather assessment data regarding student and faculty perceptions of instructional sessions and information literacy. They are also appealing because their results can be easily summarized and conveyed to faculty, students, administrators, and other stakeholders. Although surveys are limited in what they can ask of respondents, they facilitate large-scale data gathering.

Surveys can produce results that are more representative of the population in which we are interested than other data gathering techniques. This feature is important when we want to understand something about a large population. By surveying a well-chosen sample of the population, we can generalize the results to the larger population. For example, if we want to find out how seniors feel about the usefulness of library instruction sessions, we can survey a sample of seniors. If that sample is representative of the entire senior class, we can apply the results to the whole class.

When considering whether a sample is representative, it is important to look not only at sample size, but also at the general characteristics of the sample (for example, is the percentage of the sample who are women proportional to the overall percentage of women in the senior class?). The characteristics to consider depend on the topic of the survey. For a survey on information literacy, we might be interested in students' majors, whether English is their first language, their grade point averages overall and in their majors, whether they are transfer students, or whether they live on campus, off-campus, or commute. We're looking for characteristics that might affect a student's responses to the survey questions.

A key benefit to using surveys is the familiarity that most students and faculty have with them. Very little orientation is necessary, and the validity of results can be improved as a result of the comfort level that many respondents have with the survey format. It is also easy not only to maintain anonymity with survey instruments, but also to demonstrate the anonymity of the process, thereby encouraging honest responses.

A significant drawback to using surveys is the challenge of getting enough people to respond. Most of us, especially students, are inundated with requests for feedback—even trips to the store include a survey request on the receipt these days. Therefore, it can be difficult to get students or faculty to respond to our surveys. Incentives are often used to encourage response, but they can be costly and time- and labor-intensive to implement.

Despite the potential time, effort, and expense involved, surveys are an effective tool for gathering data from your target audience. They can be used to assess information literacy at any setting, but are most often used at the programmatic or institutional level.

PRACTICAL CONSIDERATIONS

Three practical considerations for conducting your survey involve who and when you survey, how you deliver the survey, and what types of questions you ask.

Who and When

Surveys may be defined by the time period or sequence of data collection. A cross-sectional survey is used when you want to collect information at one point in time and the sample is drawn from a predetermined population. This is the most common type of survey.

A longitudinal survey is used to collect data at different points in time to study changes over time. These studies involve considerably more expense and commitment but are ideal for finding out if new programs, changes in instructional approaches, or other initiatives are having an impact. It's important to design these surveys carefully because you should plan to ask the same questions every year. If you make significant changes to the questions, you will not be able to compare results from one year to the next. Write, pretest, and revise the survey questions until you are completely satisfied with them.

There are three types of longitudinal studies:

Trend studies. A given section of the general population is sampled at each data-collection point, but the same individuals are not surveyed each time. Each sample represents the same population.

Example: Incoming freshmen at a university are surveyed every fall.

Cohort studies. A specific population is followed over a period of time. The population remains the same, but different individuals are sampled from one data collection point to another.

Example: Samples of students who began as new freshmen at a university in fall 2007 are surveyed every fall until they graduate.

Panel studies. A sample is selected at the outset of the study and the same individuals are surveyed each time. With panel studies there is loss of subjects over time, particularly as the years go by and participants make major changes in their lives, such as graduating from college.

Example: A sample of the same 500 freshmen at a university is surveyed every September for 10 years.

Survey Delivery

There are several ways that self-administered questionnaires may be distributed and returned. Paper and pencil surveys are usually mailed to participants, then completed and mailed back, but such surveys can also be distributed, completed, and returned on-site. Computerized questionnaires are being used more frequently. An example is the LIBQUAL+™ survey, in which an e-mail is sent to the target population with a link to the online survey. If you want to survey students enrolled in distance learning courses, an online survey is the practical choice. In fact, if you want to minimize the effort needed by students to respond to your survey, an online survey is superior to paper and pencil almost every time. An exception might be a classroom setting, where a paper survey can be distributed, completed, and collected efficiently without the need for computers.

There are several online survey systems available. These systems can help a great deal with distribution of the survey, keeping track of responses, and compiling data. They can also help you by giving your survey a clean and professional look. Two of the more popular ones are SurveyMonkey.com and Flashlight Online (The TLT Group, 2007) (www.tltgroup.org/Flashlight/flashlightonline.htm). The basic version of SurveyMonkey is free and allows you to ask up to 10 questions and receive up to 100 responses. The responses that you get from SurveyMonkey do need to be coded if you want to conduct any additional statistical analyses with a program such as SPSS. The advanced version, with more features and more questions and responses allowed, requires a monthly subscription. Flashlight Online, offered by The TLT Group, offers many question and response options. Data from Flashlight are coded and ready to use with statistical software programs. According to The TLT Group Web site, "Flashlight Online is normally available only through institutional site license and only to institutions with site licenses for Flashlight tools. If your institution has paid for Flashlight Online, you can get a free account." To use this product, you will need to find out if your institution has a site license.

Survey Questions

Whether you use an online survey system or not, you will have to write your survey questions. This section provides some background information about survey items. Figure 6.1 lists four types of question/response pairings and Figure 6.2 defines the types of response options. Many of those options will be familiar. The important thing is not that you know what each option is called, but that you are knowledgeable enough about each type to make the best choices for your survey items. The next section offers guidelines for writing good survey questions.

Question Open—Response Open: Question is of a general nature and there are no fixed response options.
Example: *How do you feel about the library orientation program?*

Question Open—Response Closed: Question is of a general nature and a fixed list of possible responses is presented.
Example: *How do you feel about the library orientation program?*

> *It was valuable.*
> *It was helpful.*
> *It was not a good use of my time.*
> *It was not useful.*

Question Closed—Response Open: The question is more specific but respondents write in responses.
Example: *What did you learn in the library orientation that you will use right away?*

Question Closed—Response Closed: The question is more specific and there are a limited number of responses from which to choose.
Example: *What did you learn in the library orientation that you will use right away?*

> *How to find books.*
> *How to find journal articles.*
> *How to get help.*

Figure 6.1. Types of Question/Response Pairings.

Dichotomous: Two choices.
Examples: *True/False*
              Yes/No

Multiple Choice: More than two choices; respondents choose one answer.
Examples: *Yes/No/Don't know*
              Once a week/Once a month/Once a semester/Never

Checklist: Respondents check off as many as apply.
Examples:

              How to find books.
              How to find journal articles.
              How to use the databases.
              How to get help.

Rating Scale: Respondents indicate intensity, frequency, degree of interest, degree of agreement.
Examples:

              Strongly agree   agree   disagree   strongly disagree
              Very much   somewhat   very little

Semantic Differential: A combination of a rating scale and a checklist.
Examples:

              Good _ _ _ _ _ _ _ _ _ _ _ Bad
              Frequently _ _ _ _ _ _ _ _ _ Infrequently
              Often _ _ _ _ _ _ _ _ _ _ _ Rarely

Figure 6.2. Types of Response Options.

STEPS FOR CONDUCTING A SURVEY

The steps below will guide you through the process of planning and implementing a survey. We include tips for writing good items; organizing and distributing the survey; and sharing results. We also offer numerous ideas for increasing your response rate.

1. Define the Survey Objectives

To help focus your survey, answer the following questions:

What are you trying to find out? Be very specific. For example, "I want to know if students value the library orientation class and tour immediately afterward. I also want to know if students value the library orientation later in the semester."

What is your time frame? Are you interested in current practices or in trends over time? This will determine if you do a cross-sectional or longitudinal study.

Who is your population of interest? Whose opinions or behaviors are you interested in?

Whose opinions matter to the project? Who can be reached, given the resources available? Connecting with your target group may take some resourcefulness and collaboration with faculty or others. If you will rely on others to reach your sample, you should begin right away to make contact with them. You should explain the purpose of your survey, what role you wish them to play, and perhaps invite suggestions or comments on the survey design, questions, or implementation.

What specifically do you need to know from your respondents? This leads to one of the core rules for surveys, which is to be selective about what questions you include on your survey. Ask only what is essential to the purpose of your project. You do not want to waste the time of respondents (and having fewer questions means more people will be willing to respond). It takes some discipline to keep to the essential questions, but it will be well worth the effort. A quick check to determine the importance of a question is to ask yourself what you will do with the information. If you're asking a question "just out of curiosity," that question is not essential.

2. Write the Survey Items

Keep in mind that survey respondents are expected to answer questions without any intervention from you. Therefore, the items should be self-contained and easily understood. Figure 6.3 offers essential tips on writing good survey items.

Once you have written all your questions, consider whether some of the them can be converted to a different item type to save space and to help the respondent by offering a consistent set of response options. This may be as simple as condensing a number of questions with separate responses to a checklist or rating scale. See Figure 6.4 for an example.

Short surveys, of five questions or fewer, are fairly easy to write. Longer surveys need a bit more attention to things like how the questions flow, grouping similar types of items (like checklists) together, and guiding respondents through the survey.

3. Construct the Survey

The main things to consider when putting your survey together are the overall layout, the instructions, and the ordering of the items. Keep in mind that most surveys are completed without any intervention with respondents, so they must be easy to understand and complete or the response rate may be too low to be useful.

Overall, the survey should be attractive, with items and pages numbered. The name and address of the person who is to receive the completed survey should appear prominently. Questions should be organized and laid out so that the survey is easy to complete.

The survey should be as short as possible and still be consistent with the objectives of the study. Completion is affected by respondents' motivation, perception of usefulness of the survey, how easy or complicated the questions are to answer, and any incentives offered.

Instructions should be brief and clear and must stand out so that they are easy to find. Examples may be used to show how to complete the items or for any items that might be confusing. Brief information about the purpose of the survey should be included. It is helpful to include information about how long the survey will take to complete (which may be estimated from the pretest, as discussed below). It must be clear to respondents what they are to do with the survey once they have completed it. Include a "thank-you" statement either with the instructions or at the end.

Ordering of items should follow some logical sequence. Put questions about the same topic together. When moving to a new topic, it may be helpful to use a transitional sentence. If the survey is long, do not put important items at the end, as respondents might give up before reaching those questions. You can use "filter" or "skip" questions to help the respondent move through more quickly. For example, you might ask, "*Did your English class go to the library this semester for a presentation by a librarian? If yes, please answer the next five questions, #6 through #10. If no, please skip to question #11.*"

- Use standard English; avoid jargon, slang, and abbreviations.

- Make questions concrete. That is, refer to specific places, events, locations, entities. You may even need to provide a reminder before the questions. For example, *"Earlier this semester, a librarian came to your English 10002 class and taught a session on using library resources. How do you rate the effectiveness of the librarian's instruction?"* Not, *"What did you think about the librarian?"*

- Specify the time period to be considered. For example, *"In the last month, how often have you used a research database, such as Academic Search Premier, to find articles in magazines or journals?"*

- Offer a "don't know" or "no opinion" option. Respondents should always have an option that is right for them. If you are asking them to recall something, they might not know the answer so the "don't know" option will let them answer the question accurately. This is particularly important if you are using an online survey that requires a response to each question before moving on. Be careful not to force a respondent to choose an incorrect answer, which will have a negative effect on your results and interpretation of the data.

  If the topic of the survey is of little importance to your target group, you may get many "no opinion" responses. Some survey makers will leave out the "no opinion" option, thereby forcing respondents to select an opinion. This approach can be useful if you have a range of possible answers (not just *"really loved it"* and *"really hated it"*) and when you want to get a general sense of how your target group as a whole feels about something.

- Each question should have just one thought. Avoid double-barreled questions that really ask two things. For example, avoid questions like, *"Was the instructor for this session well-organized and effective in presenting the material?"* What if the instructor was well-organized, but not clear in presentation? The respondent will not be able to give you an accurate answer. It is better to separate the two concepts and allow a response to each.

- Avoid leading questions that hint for a certain response, for example, *"The library assigned five librarians full-time to planning and giving orientation tours this term because we consider teaching freshmen about core library services very important. Do you think that the orientation tour was useful?"*

- Avoid asking for unusually detailed information, for example, *"In the past year how many times have you asked for library help to find information? What was the topic of each question you asked? Did you ask in-person, by phone, by e-mail, by chat, or through another medium?"*

- When asking for opinions, offer balanced response options that have equal numbers of positive and negative responses. For example, avoid sets of response options like, *"excellent, pretty good, good, poor"* which has three positive options and one negative option.

- <u>Items that are interesting and clearly relevant to the study will increase response rate.</u>

Figure 6.3. Tips for Writing Good Survey Items.

Original questions and responses

1. How do you rate this instructor's organizational skills?
   Disorganized   Poorly organized   No opinion   Somewhat organized   Very organized
2. How do you rate this instructor's presentation skills?
   Excellent   Good   Fair   Poor
3. The instructional material was effective.
   Strongly agree   Agree   No opinion   Disagree   Strongly disagree

After conversion

Please indicate whether you agree with each statement.

	Strongly Agree	Agree	No Opinion	Disagree	Strongly Disagree
The instructor was well organized.	O	O	O	O	O
The instructor demonstrated good presentation skills.	O	O	O	O	O
The instructional material was not effective.	O	O	O	O	O

One caveat with this type of condensing is that respondents may be tempted to simply go down the page and mark the same answer for every item. You can discourage this by making some statements positive and some negative, which requires that respondents read each statement carefully and respond separately to each.

Figure 6.4. Example of Condensing Items.

4. Conduct a Pretest

A pretest is essential for determining whether your survey is well constructed and if your procedures for distribution and return are adequate. Ideally, the techniques you use for administering the pretest should be the same as those planned for the real data collection. However, at the very least, several people from your target population should be asked to complete the survey and provide any feedback on items as well as the overall survey. It may be helpful if the pretest form provides space for respondents to make comments. You may need to make revisions to your survey based on this feedback.

5. Prepare a Letter or Message of Transmittal

If you are sending out your survey by U.S. mail or e-mail, you should include a brief cover letter that explains the purpose of your survey and to urge a response. Altruistic and egoistic appeals can help to convince respondents to participate (for example, *"Your responses will help us improve our instruction. We will also learn more about your information needs."*).

Give some thought as to who the letter will be from. Asking a department chair, faculty member, the library director, or other university administrator to originate the letter or cosign with you can convey to respondents the importance of participating. The cover letter can be an important factor in increasing your response rate.

You may also offer to make the results available after the data have been summarized. A date for return of the survey should be included.

6. Conduct the Initial Distribution and Follow-Up

For surveys that are mailed, contacting the target group prior to sending the actual survey increases response rates. This can be a simple e-mail or postcard alerting the group that a survey is on its way and asking for their participation when it comes.

Once your survey is ready, send it out. Be sure to include instructions for returning the survey and the deadline. It is best to give respondents at least a week and no more than two weeks to respond. You should extend that time if you are surveying over a holiday. Then, unless your response rate is unusually high, you should send a follow-up request. It is often helpful (although costly, if you are using U.S. mail) to send a different letter of transmittal with another copy of the survey because the original copy of the survey may have been lost or thrown away. A cheaper, though less effective, option is to send a postcard reminder. If the original distribution was via e-mail, the follow-up should also be by e-mail. If you are tracking responses returned (see below), you can target your follow-up to nonrespondents.

7. Track Responses

Tracking returned surveys requires considerable forethought and is time consuming, but it allows more targeted follow-up and a more exact method for examining nonresponses. Tracking means keeping track of who has responded to the survey (and therefore, who has not responded). For surveys that collect sensitive information, such as risky health behaviors, there are a number of techniques to ensure anonymity of responses, which will reassure participants and increase response rates. For surveys on information literacy topics, less extreme measures of anonymity can be used. You should inform participants that their responses will be anonymous. If you are tracking responses, which we recommend, you can let respondents know that you are doing so to ensure a representative sample and that you will not record who has responded in what way.

To track responses to an online survey, give each member of your target group a unique identifier in the original e-mail that invites them to participate. Each respondent will type that identifier in the survey (which means, of course, that the survey must have a field for the identifier). More sophisticated online systems can assign a unique identifier to each participant which they use to login to the survey.

For paper surveys sent via U.S. mail, you can place a unique identifier on the survey or on a return envelope that will be destroyed when the completed survey is received.

Maintain a list of your target group members and the unique identifiers assigned to them. As you receive completed surveys, mark the list accordingly. You will know from your list who has not responded.

8. Compile Responses

Before response data can be analyzed they must be organized into some format, often a spreadsheet. The best way to begin is to take a blank copy of your survey and determine how you will represent the questions and response options. Usually the questions become variables or column headers with short, descriptive names, although even just the question number will do. Response options are often numbered from low to high. After you have marked up a blank survey form in this way, it becomes your codebook for entering and analyzing the data and understanding the results.

Responses from surveys are usually presented as frequency counts and percentages. If you have a large number of responses, percentages may be sufficient as long as somewhere in your presentation of results you mention the total number of respondents.

Results may be given for items individually, especially if your survey is short. If your survey is long or you have items grouped by topic, you may want to discuss results for several items together.

9. Determine What to do About Nonrespondents

The important question to answer regarding nonrespondents is, how would the results have changed if the entire sample had returned the survey? If your final response rate is less than 80%, it is a good idea to spend some time checking the nonresponding group to find out the answer to that question. The purpose is to find out whether their responses to the survey would be substantially different from those who did respond. Of course, getting responses from the nonrespondents can be quite a challenge! You can make it more manageable by focusing on a small portion (around 10%) of the nonrespondents. You first need to decide who is a nonrespondent (for example, anyone who did not respond either to the initial survey or to the follow-up contact).

You can target these final nonrespondents with contacts by e-mail, postcard, or letter. Or, you can try to contact them by telephone and ask them the survey questions while you are talking with them. As you reach these people and get responses, keep their responses separate from the original responding group. When you have enough information from this group, you should compare their survey responses to the original group's. Figure 6.5 shows an example comparing responses of both groups.

You can see that the nonrespondents had a lower opinion than the original group. Your challenge at this point would be to see if you can figure out why the nonrespondents had these lower opinions. Do they share some common characteristic that could explain this result?

If the nonrespondents differ substantially from the original respondents, you have two options. You can pursue more of the nonrespondents and add their responses to your tabulations, which means your ultimate results will more accurately reflect your entire target group. Or, you can acknowledge that your results are <u>not</u> representative of the target group.

10. Share Results with Respondents

At the very least, make the results of the survey available to those who responded or were asked to respond. This allows those who took the time to complete your survey to know that their feedback was used and valued. It also follows through on any interest that you sparked among your respondents by showing those interested how their responses fit in among the responses of the larger population.

Even a simple tabulation will do for sharing results. Once you have the results tabulated, compile a simple report and post it online. See Chapter 13 for more on analyzing the results and Chapter 14 for tips on sharing assessment results. You can

Original responding group's responses	Nonrespondents' eventual responses
excellent—70%	excellent—20%
good—20%	good—40%
fair—8%	fair—20%
poor—2%	poor—20%

Figure 6.5. Example of Differences in Group Responses.

announce the availability of the results using the same communication vehicle (for example, a departmental listserv) that you used to ask for participants.

ARE SURVEYS RIGHT FOR YOU?

Review the following factors when considering surveys:

  Time

With the advent of online survey systems, time is less of a factor when considering surveys than it used to be. Online surveys considerably decrease the amount of time it takes to distribute the survey, monitor the response rate, and tabulate the responses. The bulk of your time will be spent developing the items to be included on the survey and pre-testing the instrument to make sure that it makes sense to respondents and elicits the types of responses that you expect.

If you are conducting an in-house survey using paper and pencil, your time commitment will increase to include the time needed to handle the paper surveys and to tabulate the responses. In order to reach as much of your population as possible, you may need more than one communication channel, which also increases your time commitment as coordinating the distribution of the online and paper surveys at the same time can be more time consuming, and merging responses into a usable format can also require considerable effort.

$$ Money

Money can be a factor to consider. Your costs will increase somewhat if you are using a paper and pencil survey to cover the expense for materials. If you will be mailing your survey to respondents, costs will also increase to cover mailing costs not only for distributing the survey, but for the return postage and follow-up mailings.

Using an online system will considerably decrease the costs of surveying. Many institutions subscribe to survey services, such as Flashlight Online, or host their own for no-cost use by departments on campus.

Your costs will also increase if you use an incentive to encourage students or faculty to participate. Periodic or single raffles are common incentives used to encourage participation. Because many students are inundated with survey participation requests, incentives need to be appealing and to stand out, which often means they can be expensive.

 Level of Assessment

Surveys can be used for any level of assessment. You can use a survey to assess how students reacted to a particular classroom session or experience, the impact of your instructional program on a department's curriculum, or the state of information literacy on your campus. As you move from classroom assessment to institutional assessment using surveys, your time and financial commitments will likely increase. However, surveys can be an effective tool for gathering feedback from a significant sample of your student or faculty population.

 ### Assessment Domain

Surveys are best used to assess at the affective level. For classroom assessment, you can include a few items designed to measure whether the students retained key points of the session; however, if you are truly interested in assessing at the cognitive level, other tools such as knowledge tests and concept mapping are more suited to that purpose.

As an assessment tool, surveys are most effectively used to measure how students and faculty feel about your instruction or instructional program. You can also use surveys to gather information in general. For example, if you are unsure of how information literacy is taught by faculty from outside of the library, you can survey those colleagues to gain a more complete perspective of the information literacy environment on campus.

 ### Access to Participants

If you are conducting a survey during an information literacy session, you have ready access to participants. If the survey is given outside of class, however, you will have to put some effort into identifying your target group and figuring out how to reach them. Is there a departmental listserv you can use? Are there ready-made e-mail or mailing lists? Depending on the scale of your project, you may need to seek help from faculty, department chairs, or your school's institutional research office or assessment office.

 ### Level of Faculty Collaboration

Faculty collaboration, while not absolutely necessary for surveys, is highly recommended. In all likelihood you will be assessing at the programmatic or institutional level, which surely involves faculty. Because they are stakeholders they will have an interest in your assessment results. Collaboration here at the very least will give faculty a sense of inclusion, and they can also be valuable contributors during the planning process. As mentioned above, they can also be helpful in recruiting participants. Of course, if you are surveying faculty, their collaboration will be essential.

 ### Outside Expertise

Your need for outside expertise depends on your own comfort level and the availability of assistance from your colleagues. It is likely that someone in the library has previous survey experience that you can build on for your project. Also, many academic departments, such as sociology, marketing, and business, have people with expertise in survey design, administration, and data analysis.

If you do design your survey from scratch, remember to follow the steps above, particularly the pre-testing of your questions. You can also consult the materials listed in the bibliography for many more helpful tips.

Creating an online survey, if you choose that method, can require additional technical skills. Your university's systems department may be able to help.

WORKS CITED AND FURTHER READING

Biemer, P. P. and Lyberg, L. (2003). *Introduction to survey quality*. Hoboken, NJ: Wiley.

Czaja, R. and Blair, J. (2005). *Designing surveys: A guide to decisions and procedures* (2nd ed.). Thousand Oaks, CA: Pine Forge Press.

Fink, A. (2003). *The survey kit* (2nd ed.). Thousand Oaks, CA: Sage Publications.

Fink, A. (2006). *How to conduct surveys: A step-by-step guide* (3rd ed.). Thousand Oaks, CA: Sage Publications.

Powell, R. R. and Connaway, L. S. (2004). *Basic research methods for librarians* (4th ed.). Westport, CT: Libraries Unlimited.

Survey design. (2005). *The survey system's tutorial*. Petaluma, CA: Creative Research Systems. www.surveysystem.com/sdesign.htm.

SurveyMonkey.com. (2006). http://surveymonkey.com/.

The TLT Group. (2007). *The Flashlight program*. www.tltgroup.org/Flashlight/flashlightonline.htm.

7

Interviewing

Indicators:

 Requires a significant time commitment

$ Requires little money unless outside expertise is needed

Level of assessment: Programmatic

Domain: Affective

 Access to participants: Requires medium level of effort

Faculty collaboration not required but helpful and recommended

Outside expertise may be helpful if in-house skill and experience are not available

Key Characteristics:

- Assesses how respondents think and feel through one-on-one questioning and listening.
- Takes advantage of peoples' natural inclination to discuss things.
- Strong choice for evaluating new or changing programs.
- More than other methods, it allows for the deep exploration of questions and issues.
- Works well to explore questions raised by prior assessments.
- Results, shaped by the voices of actual participants, are powerful and understandable.
- Requires interpersonal skills and experience in conducting interviews.
- Requires a great deal of time to conduct interviews.
- Not a good choice for assessing knowledge-based outcomes.

AN OVERVIEW OF INTERVIEWING

Interviewing allows us to access the hearts and minds of our students and colleagues by asking them how they think and feel and listening carefully to their responses. Interviewing can produce results that are powerful and understandable, the type of results that are easily digested and understood by students, faculty, administrators, and others outside the library. Yet interviewing is an under-used method for assessing information literacy instruction and programming. Other less time-consuming methods such as surveys and focus groups are often preferred. However, interviewing can produce much deeper and richer results than either of these methods and is effective in studying the perceptions and feelings of course and program participants. This is especially true of new courses and programs in which everyone from administrators to students may be looking for validation or understanding of how things are working.

Interviews are usually conducted face-to-face, but can be done by telephone. Some forms of interviewing are similar to survey research in that a questionnaire is used. While surveys ask respondents to record their own responses, interviewing asks respondents to speak their responses and expand upon them. Interview responses are gathered by audio or video recording, usually supplemented by note taking.

In working with the ACRL's *Information Literacy Competency Standards for Higher Education* (2000), interviewing may be useful in assessing outcomes that begin with these words: *explores, realizes, considers, investigates, assesses,* and *reflects.* Because of its ability to delve deeply into the personal and cultural influences that inform students' critical faculties, interviewing may be particularly useful in assessing Standard Three: "The information literate student evaluates information and its sources critically and incorporates selected information into his or her knowledge base and value system."

TYPES OF INTERVIEWING

Informal Interviewing

An informal interview is spontaneous and conversational. The researcher uses no predetermined questions. Questions are generated by an event or context, and subsequent questions flow from initial responses. The informal interviewer will often simply jot down notes when he or she gets back to the office after the interview has occurred. Rarely identified in formal assessment reports, the results of informal interviews are more important for gauging how participants are responding to a lesson or a task, or for finding out what the faculty member thought of the class's library session. Informal questioning is further discussed in Chapter 4, "Informal Assessment Techniques."

Guided Interviewing

This method makes use of an interview guide, or a list of suggested topics to be explored during the interview (Patton 1990, p. 283). The interviewer may word questions how he or she wishes and is free to build conversations around issues, with the advantage of being able to explore and probe specific lines of questioning. While it can be used for one-on-one interviewing, this approach is more commonly used for focus groups. See Chapter 8 on focus groups for more information.

Open-Ended Interviewing

Open-ended interviewing is the most appropriate type of interviewing for assessing library programs and the remainder of this chapter focuses largely on this type of interviewing. Open-ended interviewing uses a predetermined set of open-ended questions, carefully worded and arranged, that is administered to each respondent. This standardized question list limits flexibility in questioning, but it has a strong upside. Standardized questions can help establish reliability and also provide transparency to administrators and others who may evaluate your work. In addition, standardized questioning facilitates standardized data collection and makes analysis easier (Patton 1990, p. 285).

From this point on in the chapter, when the term interviewing is used, we are referring to open-ended interviewing.

PREPARING FOR A SUCCESSFUL INTERVIEW

The following are key questions you will need to answer to successfully prepare for conducting your interview.

What do you want your respondents to tell you?

Your learning or project outcomes should directly inform your answer to this question. While question design is covered in Chapter 6 on surveys, consider these five types of questions for your interview list:

1. Behavior Questions ask about past experiences, behaviors, and activities that would have been observable had an observer been present.

   Examples: Can you walk me through your last experience searching the library catalog?

   How did your class behave during the research database assignment we designed for your lesson?

2. Values Questions ask about what people think or what their opinions are on topics or issues. They can reveal people's goals and desires.

   Examples: Which do you like better, Google or the library's information resources? Why?

   What would you like to see happen with library instruction for students enrolled in English composition?

3. Feeling Questions ask how people feel. They seek to explore the emotions of people regarding their thoughts and experiences. Feeling questions are often confused with opinion questions. Take care in phrasing your questions and be certain whether you are asking about what people think or what they feel (Patton 1990, p. 291).

   Examples: How did you feel during the library instruction session your class attended?

   The next time you used the library after you took the library tour, how did you feel?

4. Knowledge Questions ask people to recall a fact or make a decision based on their knowledge. These types of questions can be used to measure awareness of available services or resources. Be careful when asking questions about knowledge or skills. These questions often need some

context to avoid threatening your respondent. For example, you might let respondents know that their responses will be used only to evaluate the program or class. This can help respondents to understand that they are not the ones being judged or evaluated. Also, these types of questions will work best after rapport and trust have been established in the interview.

> Examples: What avenues for research help are available at this library?
>
> What options are available in the library catalog for searching for materials by topic?

5. <u>Background Questions</u> identify the characteristics of the person being interviewed. Carefully consider what information you already know about your respondents and what additional background information you may need. Sometimes background information can also be compiled by using a brief survey before or after the interview.

> Examples: What is your age?
>
> What is your major?

Have you considered the time frame and order of your questions?

You can ask any of the five types of questions in the past tense, present tense, or future tense. The five question types across the three time dimensions create the possibility of 15 different questions, but you should avoid asking questions in all these categories. Do not draw up a tedious, lengthy interview that may turn off respondents (Patton 1990, p. 293).

The order of questions can be important to your interview. Consider the following suggestions:

- Start with straightforward, descriptive questions about present behaviors. Such questions are noncontroversial and respondents will be able to give direct responses that may set them at ease. Gentle follow-up questions can help establish rapport.
- After gathering descriptive information, you are positioned to ask questions related to feelings and opinions. By having the respondents first describe their experiences, they will more likely be able to recall their corresponding feelings. This will allow your respondents to ground their feelings within the context of their experiences.
- Questions about the present are best at the beginning, followed by questions reflecting on the past. Questions about the future, which can produce speculative answers, usually work better later in the interview.
- If you are including background questions, they should be sprinkled throughout your interview. Respondents find these questions boring and sometimes intrusive, so it is best not to overwhelm respondents with these questions. They usually work best in the second half of interviews.

Are your questions worded properly?

The way a question is worded can greatly affect how your interviewees respond. Focus on creating questions that are open-ended, neutral, clear, and focused on a single topic. Watch out for leading, confusing, and very long questions.

How will you record your responses?

You can record responses simply by taking notes, but a recording device is recommended to make sure all responses are captured accurately. A handheld tape recorder will usually suffice, but make sure you test it immediately prior to beginning your interview to verify that it is in working order. Also, have a backup power supply and extra batteries on hand just in case.

How will you enlist your respondents?

You will be targeting students or colleagues within the program you plan to assess, but how will you access them? Will you recruit independently or in collaboration with faculty or staff? Will you offer incentives or snacks to participants? For a full discussion of recruiting participants, please refer to Chapter 8 on focus groups, where specific recruiting approaches are described.

Once you have a list of potential participants, you will need to contact them, screen them, and schedule their appointments. It is a good idea to create a script to guide your interactions. You should include the purpose of your interview, the criteria for the respondents' inclusion in the project, their role, and their options for setting an appointment. Remember, when working with people for research purposes, you will also need to have respondents give their consent to your interview. It is a good idea to mention this up front to avoid surprising or misleading your respondents.

When and where will the interview be conducted?

This relates closely to the previous question. Consider times that are convenient to respondents. Remember, if respondents feel put out or bothered, they are less likely to cooperate and speak openly. When selecting a location, look for a nonthreatening place that is comfortable and familiar. If the location requires scheduling, reserve the room for at least an hour and a half. Interviews usually last about an hour, but leave yourself extra time for setting up the interview and wrap-up activities.

Who will interview them?

This is an important question. First, consider if you or your colleagues possess the appropriate skills and expertise, or whether you need to turn to an outside expert. The following description will give you an idea of what you are looking for. A skilled interviewer can take advantage of the dynamics of face-to-face communication to:

- Easily and quickly establish rapport, setting the interviewee at ease.
- Ask for clarification when needed.
- Redirect and refocus the interview discussion as needed.
- Maintain a neutral and interested demeanor that encourages frank discussion.
- Explore and dig deeply into key questions and issues with pointed follow-up questions.
- Note key nonverbal behaviors that can be used to supplement the interviewee's responses.

Second, consider how many interviewers you need. A large-scale interview of multiple respondents may require multiple interviewers. This will require that interviewers be trained and coached in advance of the interviews. In smaller interviews, keep the number of interviewers to a minimum. Different interviewers will have different styles, making data comparison more problematic. If possible, consider using a single interviewer to make data analysis easier and the interpretation more reliable. Also, we recommended that you (or the interviewer) conduct a few practice interviews before meeting with respondents. This will help to make your delivery smooth and to point out potential problem areas in the interview.

When you have answered all these questions, you are ready to conduct the interview. Figure 7.1 offers advice for making the interview flow smoothly and be productive. Figure 7.2 is an example of an interview, including the interview planning and preparation process and the interview script.

RIGHT AFTER THE INTERVIEW

Make sure you got what you needed. If you used a tape recorder, check to see that it worked properly. If you used note taking, go over your notes and flesh out anything that is unclear while your memories are fresh.

Take time now to record your observations during the interview. Did the respondent appear nervous or anxious at any point? Were there any surprises? What worked? What did not work? You should also include standard elements, like the date, place, and time of the interview. We recommended that you create a post-interview form to lead you and other interviewers through this observational recording process.

TRANSCRIBING THE DATA

Data transcription can be a time-consuming process. One hour of recorded audio can take up to four hours to transcribe (Patton 1990, p. 349). With this in mind, data transcription and the analysis that will follow should be considered early in the planning process. Below are some key considerations and recommendations for transcribing interview data.

- If using a tape recorder, verify that it is working properly.

- Ask one question at a time. This will help avoid confusing respondents.

- Attempt to remain as neutral as possible, while at the same time being supportive.

- Use verbal and nonverbal cues to encourage responses (a nod of the head, phraseology like, "Yes, go on").

- When taking notes, do not cause distractions by letting it slow down the pace of the interview.

- Do not reveal your reaction to responses by quickly starting to scribble notes. Remain calm and cool.

- Provide transition between major topics. Avoid jumping from topic to topic. Tell respondents when you are switching to a new topic.

- Watch your time and do not lose control of the interview. Watch for respondents straying off the subject or giving long answers. You may need to cut short some responses in order to get through the whole interview within your time limits. Also, if respondents begin to ask questions, try to hold these off until the interview has been completed.

Figure 7.1. Tips for Conducting the Interview.

The following sample interview provides an overview of an assessment scenario and the interview planning and preparation process. The interview script, including the question list, is included.

The Assessment Scenario

Conduct a follow-up interview of participants in an information literacy workshop six months after the conclusion of the workshop to:

1. Evaluate the workshop as an evolving program.
2. Understand the values and perceptions of participants.
3. Explore variations among participants' experiences.

The interviews will contribute data to the overall assessment of the program. Of particular interest will be the comparison of the participants' interview responses with their survey responses provided at the final workshop meeting.

Program Description: Information Literacy Workshop for Bridge Program

   Librarians delivered an information literacy workshop to 28 students as part of a summer "bridge" program. The summer program brings incoming freshmen to campus during the summer for eight weeks, during which they take two required liberal arts classes and a series of workshops. The information literacy workshop consisted of four two-hour meetings in the library. A lesson plan was created for each meeting, and each lesson had specific learning objectives. The overall objectives focused on identifying information needs, identifying information sources, evaluating information, and the ethical use of information. Additional goals of the workshop included orienting students to the library and helping students recognize the value of the library to their success as students. This was the first time the workshop was offered and it is an evolving component of the library's instruction program for first-year students.

The Interview Plan

The Interview: Formal interviews with standardized, open-ended questions will be conducted with eight workshop participants.

Interviewer: A colleague from the library's instruction team, whom the participants do not know, will serve as interviewer. The interviewer was fully briefed on the workshop and practiced the interview with one of the library's student workers.

Access to Participants: Students in the summer bridge program continue to meet during the semester for study halls and other programming. The director of the program has agreed to allow students to participate in interviews during their study halls.

Interview Location: The interviews will be conducted during the early evenings in the lounge of the campus life student center, in the immediate vicinity of the study halls. The lounge is quiet at that time of day, and the interviewer and interviewees should be comfortable talking around a table in the corner.

Recording Device: The interviewer will use a mini tape recorder during the interviews. Extra batteries and tapes will be on hand.

Note Taking: The interviewer will have a clipboard holding a copy of the interview script and question list. Each copy will be used as a form also. On it the interviewer will record the time, date and place of the interview, along with the interviewee's name. The interviewer will also use space between questions to note follow-up questions and to jot down quick observations.

Post Interview: The interviewer will complete a post-interview processing form that records additional observations and the interviewer's own perceptions. The interviewer will attach this form to the interview script and notes taken during the interview.

Transcribing Data: Librarians will later transcribe the audio recordings of the interviews, entering the data into a Microsoft Excel spreadsheet.

Analyzing Data: The librarians will perform a content analysis, first by comparing different responses to the same questions and second by comparing interview responses to earlier responses from the survey.

Interview Script and Question List

Date: _____   Time: _____

Location: _____

Respondent's Name: _____

Introduction: Hello. Thanks for meeting with me. I want to talk with you for a few minutes today about the library and the library workshop you participated in during the summer.

1. But first, let me ask, how has your semester been going?
2. How is life in the dorms? (May include other small talk. Your purpose here is to break the ice and establish rapport.)

Transition: Okay, now I'm going ask some more serious questions.

3. How many times have you used the library this semester?
4. Can you walk me through your most recent experience in the library?
5. How do you feel now when you walk into the library?
6. Can you tell me about the last time you used the library to find information? (Do not include if respondent already cited such an experience.)
7. Would you consider it a successful experience? (Again, not needed if respondent already answered this.)
8. How did that experience make you feel? (Not needed if respondent already answered this.)
9. Have you received any additional library instruction since the library workshop?
10. If so, can you tell me about this experience?

Transition: Now I'm going to ask a few questions that will help the library evaluate the effectiveness of the workshop. I want to stress that these questions are not meant to judge you, but to help us evaluate the usefulness of the workshop.

11. Did you attend all the meetings of the workshop?
12. If you needed help finding information, where would you turn? (Ask for a specific answer.)
13. If I asked you to find a journal article, what type of information resource would you turn to?

14. If I gave you the call number of a book in the library, how would you determine what floor it was on?

Transition: Well, that wasn't so bad, was it? I'd like to wrap things up by asking you to reflect on a few topics related to the workshop.

15. Looking back on the library workshop, what are your thoughts? Just tell me the first few things that come to mind.
16. Can you tell me about a time during the last six months when you've reflected on or thought about your experiences from the workshop?
17. Can you tell me about a time when you've made use of something you learned in the workshop?
18. What would you think of making the workshop available to more students in the future?
19. Can you take a few moments to describe what you think the library's role in your education is?

Closing: I've asked all of my questions. Do you have any questions for me? Thanks for your time. (Shake hands with the student.) Your experiences and thoughts will be a great help to us in improving future workshops.

Figure 7.2. Sample Interview.

What will be transcribed?

Word-for-word transcriptions are best, but require the most time. A more practical approach is to focus on "meaningful responses." By meaningful responses, we mean those utterances that make sense and are in direct response to a question or topic. This would exclude off-topic digressions, interruptions, background noises, and silences. Also, some questions may not require word-for-word transcription and responses may be summarized or categorized. For example, response to background questions can often simply be tallied. Do not forget to have the interviewer's notes transcribed as well.

What type of software will you use?

It is recommended that your data be transcribed using some type of software. This makes your data reproducible and flexible as you move forward toward analysis. Microsoft Excel is a good choice because your data can be exported easily from Excel to other software applications. Some data analysis software packages have features designed to analyze qualitative data, but you must be aware of any special formatting needs of this software before starting to transcribe your data. Refer to Chapter 13, "Analyzing the Data," for more information on data analysis software.

Who will do the transcribing?

If your budget allows, you might hire someone to transcribe your data. Maybe you have a graduate assistant who can do the work or you have the time yourself. Whoever does the transcription, he or she will need clear guidelines, including what to transcribe and how to transcribe it. He or she must be familiar with the software and file naming conventions used. He or she should also be familiar with the project and the interview questions. Once transcription is underway, it is recommended that you compare portions of the transcriptions against the audiotape to ensure accuracy.

Start transcribing data as soon as possible

As data transcription is so time consuming, it is best to start on it as soon as an interview is over. There is no need to wait for all interviews to be completed. Working through an initial transcription can also help streamline the whole interview process by pointing out problems with questions or the interviewer's delivery.

ANALYZING THE DATA

Once your transcriptions are complete, you are ready to analyze your data. You should read through the responses and look for trends. Do you notice that many respondents expressed similar opinions about a program? If you asked for ideas or suggestions, do you have enough useful responses to generate a list? For questions that asked about unmet needs, are you able to identify those needs? The plan is that you, along with your colleagues, will be able to quickly get a sense of how your respondents think or feel about your topics.

A full discussion of data analysis is beyond the scope of this chapter, but we can note that one common method for analyzing interview data in depth is content analysis, which is described in detail in Chapter 13. Content analysis is a more systematic and objective way of examining these rich data and drawing conclusions which you can then act upon.

IS INTERVIEWING RIGHT FOR YOU?

Review the following factors when considering interviewing:

 Time

Interviewing is time intensive. Each interview can take upward of two to three hours to execute, when you include scheduling and the actual interview. In addition, analyzing and interpreting qualitative data can take a great deal of effort. The preparation of interview questions can also be time consuming. If you decide to use interviewing in an assessment project, make sure you can devote plenty of time to the process.

 Money

Apart from the time spent, interviewing can be fairly inexpensive, but this is true only if you have the skills and experience to conduct interviews and analyze qualitative data. In college and university settings, you may have inexpensive access to colleagues with expertise in these areas, but sometimes outside consultants may need to be brought in, and their fees could greatly increase your assessment costs. Incentives for participants, upgrading or purchasing recording equipment, or hiring a transcriptionist can also raise your costs. Before launching into interviews, we recommend that you plot out your entire project to discover what your expenses may be.

Level of Assessment

Interviewing is a strong choice for assessing programs, especially for new and evolving programs in which participants and instructors may be trying to find direction. Informal interviewing works well in classroom settings or during informal planning discussions, but formal interviewing is usually much too time intensive for assessment at the classroom level.

 Assessment Domain

Interviewing is best used to study affective outcomes—what people think and feel, their attitudes, values, and perceptions. Knowledge questions and questions asking about prior behaviors can be included and can be helpful in gaining context during interviews, but interviewing, due to its time requirements and its focus on the individual, is not strong in assessing knowledge or behavior in any systematic way.

 Access to Participants

Because interviews require face-to-face, one-on-one meetings, gaining access to and scheduling participants can be a challenge. Sometimes incentives such as food or small monetary gifts can entice students to participate. Another avenue to accessing students can be through program coordinators or faculty, who can recruit students and possibly add additional incentives (for example, extra credit). If you are studying colleagues or faculty, you may have an easier time gaining access, but scheduling can still be difficult. See the "Preparing for a Successful Interview" section of this chapter for further discussion on enlisting participants.

 Level of Faculty Collaboration

Faculty collaboration, though not absolutely necessary for interview studies, is highly recommended. In all likelihood you will be assessing at the program level, which surely involves faculty, so they are stakeholders with an interest in your assessment results. Collaboration here at the very least will give faculty a sense of inclusion, and they can be valuable contributors during the planning process. As mentioned above, they can also be helpful in recruiting participants.

 Outside Expertise

As mentioned above in our discussion of money, outside expertise can help you overcome a lack of skill and experience in conducting interviews. Do not be alarmed, however, if you lack know-how. You can learn to conduct interviews and develop the skills you need.

Outside expertise can also help with data analysis. You can draw some quick conclusions on your own, but someone with experience in interpreting interview data can provide valuable insights.

WORKS CITED AND FURTHER READING

Association of College and Research Libraries (ACRL). (2000). *Information literacy competency standards for higher education: Standards, performance indicators, and outcomes*. Retrieved May 23, 2006 from www.ala.org/ala/acrl/acrlstandards/informationliteracycompetency.htm.

Bates, J. A. (2004). Use of narrative interviewing in everyday information behavior research. *Library & Information Science Research*, *26*(1), 15.

Gubrium, J. F. and Holstein, J. A. (2002). *Handbook of interview research: Context and method*. Thousand Oaks, CA: Sage.

Patton, M. Q. (1990). *Qualitative evaluation and research methods*. Newbury Park, CA: Sage.

Patton, M. Q. (2002). *Qualitative evaluation and research methods* (3rd ed.). Thousand Oaks, CA: Sage.

Rubin, H. J. and Rubin, I. S. (1995). *Qualitative interviewing: The art of hearing*. Thousand Oaks, CA: Sage.

Zweizig, D., Johnson, D. W., Robbins, J., and Besant, M. (1996). Interviewing. *The TELL IT! manual: The complete program for evaluating library performance*. Chicago, IL: American Library Association.

8

Focus Groups

Indicators:

 Requires a medium amount of time

$ Requires some funds only if outside expertise is needed

 Level of assessment: Programmatic, Institutional

 Domain: Affective

 Access to participants: Requires considerable effort; may need collaboration from faculty or other units on campus

 Faculty collaboration not required, but helpful and recommended

 Outside expertise may be helpful if in-house skill and experience are not available

Key Characteristics:

- Takes advantage of many peoples' natural inclination to discuss things in groups.
- Assesses how students and colleagues think and feel and also invites them to examine their responses in comparison to the views of others.
- Strong choice for exploring the differences between participants' experiences and outcomes.
- Strong choice for evaluating new and changing programs.
- Works well to explore questions raised by prior assessments.
- Useful for conducting preliminary evaluation of programs (to be followed by more in-depth assessment via other methods).

- Can produce a large amount of data in a short period of time.
- Results, shaped by the voices of actual participants, are powerful and understandable.
- Not a good choice for assessing knowledge-based outcomes.
- Requires strong interpersonal and group moderation skills.

AN OVERVIEW OF FOCUS GROUPS

Focus groups or focus group interviewing takes advantage of people's natural tendency to discuss things. Through group interaction, researchers learn about the feelings, perceptions, and attitudes of participants regarding the topic under discussion. This qualitative technique has its roots in market research and has a long history of use in industry. Focus groups have become more and more common in libraries throughout the last twenty years.

A focus group is a face-to-face interview with a group of six to twelve people that focuses on a single subject or topic; it usually lasts forty-five minutes to an hour and a half (Wilcox Johnson 1996, p. 176). The purpose of focus groups is "to draw upon respondents' attitudes, feelings, beliefs, experiences, and reactions in a way in which would not be feasible using other methods" (Gibbs 1997). Separating this methodology is its ability to take advantage of interactive discussion to generate rich and in-depth responses from multiple points of view. The interaction among participants often leads to insights and opinions that may not have been discovered through methods such as interviewing or surveying (Glitz 1998, p. 1). The individual who asks the questions, the "interviewer" in a one-on-one setting, acts as the moderator of the focus group. The moderator leads the focus group using an interview guide, a list of five to eight open-ended questions or topics. Participants, recruited from a population central to the study, are asked to reflect on, react to, and discuss the questions. Focus groups are an iterative process. "Participants get to hear each other's responses and to make additional comments beyond their own original responses as they hear what other people say" (Patton 1990, p. 335). Focus groups are not concerned with reaching a consensus, but in generating information that may increase the researcher's understanding of complex processes and issues. Focus group responses are usually recorded by note taking and audio recording.

In working with the ACRL *Information Literacy Competency Standards for Higher Education* (2000), you may find focus groups useful in assessing outcomes that begin with these words: *confers*, *explores*, *realizes*, *considers*, *investigates*, *assesses*, and *reflects*. Because of its ability to delve deeply into the personal and cultural influences that inform students' critical faculties, focus groups may be particularly useful in assessing Standard Three: "The information literate student evaluates information and its sources critically and incorporates selected information into his or her knowledge base and value system" (Association of College and Research Libraries 2000).

PREPARING FOR A SUCCESSFUL FOCUS GROUP

The apparent ease with which focus groups can be conducted can mislead us and cause us to overlook the planning process. Do not fall prey to this tendency. The planning stage of a focus group project is the best time to anticipate and overcome problems before they can hinder your study. The following are key considerations for planning successful focus groups.

What do you want participants to discuss with you?

If you have decided to use a focus group for your assessment project, you probably already have a good idea what questions or topics to explore, but if this is unclear to you, return to the objectives of the program that you seek to assess. These objectives are your starting point. You might also revisit the questions that got you thinking about assessment or even why you or your colleagues initially developed the program or instruction under review. Often we make programmatic changes in response to feedback or comments made during previous assessments. Another common impetus for focus group research is to reconcile contradictions between what students say and do. For example, students might report that they are comfortable and feel prepared, yet they perform poorly on their assignments. Or, you may wish to simply explore a new idea or the results of implementing a new idea.

Considerations for Developing Your Interview Guide

Focus groups make use of an interview or discussion guide. Interview guides differ from the question lists used commonly for one-on-one interviewing in that they are much shorter and flexible and typically focus on one large idea or theme. The same set of questions should be used with each group that meets for discussion. A sample discussion guide can be found later in this chapter. Here is a short list of tips for creating your question guides:

- Define the overall focus of your focus group and return to it often. This focus will likely be a program or program component, like a class or project. It may be concerned with a specific class of library user or type of student. It may be focused on a specific skill, such as evaluating information.
- Keep it short, five to eight questions. In general, the initial question should be an icebreaker that allows participants to introduce themselves. The next question or two should focus on broad aspects of the topic under consideration, followed by more detailed questions. Remember, group discussions are comprised of taking turns talking and listening, which can be time consuming.
- Phrase the questions directly in an open-ended manner to facilitate discussion. Refer to Chapter 7 on interviewing for more information on question wording and phrasing.
- Work out follow-up prompts or questions in advance. This requires you or the moderator to antici-pate possible responses and to plan for follow-up questioning. This can make all the difference, especially for a moderator without much experience. It can relieve the moderator of too much fast thinking and allow him or her to comfortably explore and question the views of participants. These prompts can be placed on your question guide beneath the questions they follow-up on.
- Test out the questions in advance. This can be done by conducting a test focus group or by running the questions by a group of colleagues or students in advance. Even the smallest bit of feedback can help identify problems with your questions and give you a chance to revise them.

Who will moderate?

Lack of skill in moderation is often cited as the reason for unsuccessful focus groups. You have four options in selecting a moderator:

1. **The researcher can moderate**: This may be helpful in that the researcher is intimate with the topic under review and has a high level of motivation. On the other hand, the participants may

know the moderator and feel obliged to please her or him. Also, the moderator may not be objective in approach, as he or she may have a stake in the outcome of the assessment.

2. **A colleague of the researcher can moderate**: Your colleague is less likely to be intimate with the project, but also less likely to display bias.

3. **Someone outside of the library can moderate**: This approach helps eliminate bias from the moderator, but requires extra time in briefing the moderator.

4. **An outside consultant can moderate**: This approach usually ensures a high level of skill on the moderator's part, but can significantly increase your project costs. This person will also need a detailed briefing on the project.

Which type of moderator is best for you? That depends on factors like budget and perhaps the level and uses of the assessment project. Usually libraries will have no trouble conducting their focus groups using an in-house moderator, but you must guard against bias. High profile or important projects may require a professional moderator, if your budget allows.

Regardless of where your moderator comes from (in-house or outside), that person needs certain skills as listed in Figure 8.1.

If you do use someone from inside the library, training is an important consideration. Even if the person has experience, it is recommended that at least one practice session be held to "warm up" the moderator.

Where will your focus groups be held?

The ideal location for a focus group will be one that is easy to find for participants and provides a comfortable setting for discussion. The room should be warm and bright; chairs should be comfortable. You will want to think carefully about seating arrangements. The moderator should sit among the participants, who are best seated around a conference table. If you plan to have observers, they may sit away from the group, unless they are also handling the recording of the session, in which case they must be close enough to operate the recording equipment. The room's capabilities for audio and sound recording should also be considered. If you are lucky, your institution may have specially designed facilities for focus groups that are wired for recording.

How many sessions will you conduct?

How many sessions is the right number for your project? This will involve budget constraints, time issues, and your access to students. In a perfect world, Krueger

---

- Can easily establish rapport.
- Can maintain a positive, yet neutral tone.
- Can motivate participants to get involved and participate.
- Knows when to follow-up, probe, and ask for clarification.
- Has the ability not to overreact to statements (even if they seem erroneous or extreme).
- Is good at summarizing points.
- Can direct and control the group and keep off-topic digressions to a minimum.

Figure 8.1. Moderator Skills.

suggests that sessions be repeated until little new information is generated (1994, p. 88). From a practical point of view, this usually requires three or four sessions. Most importantly, review your results after each session. This will help you gauge whether more sessions may be required. If the same comments and themes surface repeatedly throughout the first two meetings, perhaps a third session will not be required. If the first two sessions generate widely varied responses, further sessions will be in order.

Who is your target population?

Before you can focus in on your participants, you must first define your target population. Your target population is the group of students or faculty at which your instructional programming has been aimed. For example, if you are assessing your library instruction program for English composition, than your target population is students enrolled in English composition classes. However, if you are looking at aspects of a larger program, such as your library instruction program for undergraduates, your target population becomes all undergraduates. Your challenge then is to recruit your focus group participants from this target population.

How many participants will you need?

Optimally, you want groups of eight to ten participants. As a rule, you will want to aim for a larger group of participants than you need. This will give you a better chance of getting the appropriate number of participants even if some individuals fail to show up. This topic will be considered further in our discussion of recruiting participants, but in general if you want ten participants to show up, you should try to schedule twelve or thirteen.

How will you recruit and schedule participants?

Recruiting participants can be one of the most time-consuming parts of the focus group process, and the answers to a number of additional questions are needed to devise a good recruitment strategy. It should be noted that the following discussion of recruiting and scheduling participants is equally helpful to those planning one-on-one interviews, as described in Chapter 7.

How will you identify and access participants?

You can approach this in a number of ways. It is important to be flexible and creative in planning your strategy. The following section summarizes four common approaches to reaching participants. You will likely use a combination of these approaches in your recruiting efforts.

1. **Contact within a course, program, or cocurricular group:** This is the most fruitful approach if it is available to you. A faculty member within a program or course can be very helpful in identifying likely participants and helping to recruit them. Often these individuals will be colleagues or at least stakeholders in your assessment project, and they will see value in supporting your work. Do not overlook collaboration with cocurricular groups and programs. These groups often have flexible schedules and sometimes can incorporate your focus groups sessions into already reserved meeting times.

2. **Direct solicitation:** Asking students if they are interested in participating may be the next step, if you have a contact who can suggest good candidates for your focus groups. However, if you do not have a contact, you first need a list or directory of potential participants. If you are working with a large target population, such as the entire undergraduate population, the student directory may be a good source. Once you have a list of potential participants, you can contact them directly with an invitation to participate by e-mail, campus mail, or telephone.

3. **Word of mouth/referrals:** Sometimes our colleagues and network of associates can offer valuable help in the recruiting process. You can provide them with fliers or promotional cards that they can pass out to potential recruits. They may already know of good candidates and can refer you to them.

4. **Advertising:** This is another approach that can be used alone or in combination with the above methods. You can make fliers, posters, library home page ads, and print ads for the student newspaper to reach out to potential participants.

How will you make it worth their while?

An important aspect of recruiting participants is offering a reward in return for their time. If your budget allows, you may offer a small monetary payment. Alternatively, you may offer an amount of free photocopying or printing. Unlike other assessment techniques where we have suggested that one incentive method is to enter all participants in a drawing for a larger prize, it is important to give some reward to every participant. Giving every member of the focus group the same incentive promotes camaraderie which is helpful to the group discussion.

Also, we strongly recommend providing refreshments to participants when they come to your session and make sure to include this information in your recruiting materials. Food and drink can also help make participants feel comfortable.

People will often choose to participate in a focus group if they feel the project is worthwhile. In your recruitment materials you can appeal to their self-interest and altruism by explaining the purpose of the study and how it will benefit them and others.

How will you select participants?

If all goes well, a number of potential participants will indicate their interest in being in one of your focus groups. As far as numbers go, you will be looking for a pool of participants large enough to produce two focus groups to get started. You may select participants as they contact you or you may want to gather a number of interested participants and then select your groups. Your approach will depend on the group composition you want. Unless your assessment is targeted at some demographic characteristic (for example, you are studying female athletes), strive for a homogeneous, balanced group. Try to include equal numbers of males and females. If your project allows, try to gather participants who do not know each other very well. Good friends often do not work well in focus groups. They may be prone to starting side conversations and may not be comfortable providing frank responses in front of each other. Also, avoid mixing students and faculty. Again, students may not be comfortable discussing certain issues with faculty present. Finally, do not try to represent <u>every</u> demographic aspect of your target population in your groups. Do not spend too much time finding that one commuter student to participate in your focus group so that the commuter aspect of your target population is represented.

With all of these factors in mind, it is a good idea to create a profile of the group composition you want and to come up with some pre-screening questions that can help you through the selection process. Keep in mind this is not an exact process, and it can be difficult, even within large populations, to find enough qualified participants. Patience will serve you well throughout the recruitment process.

Are you prepared to go through the recruiting process more than once?

Recruiting focus group participants can be an ongoing process. If your first focus groups are successful, then you may decide you are done. However, you may need to schedule more sessions than you originally planned for a number of reasons. Maybe only three participants showed up, or perhaps the groups produced a wide variety of responses. Make sure that you do not turn away potential participants too early in the process—you may need to ask them to join an add-on session. You should also be prepared to look for additional participants by revisiting some of your earlier recruiting efforts.

How will you schedule participants?

Scheduling may seem like a technicality, but if you do not take care to be clear in your instructions and sensitive to the needs of your participants, you may not have a good showing. Here are some key considerations for scheduling:

- Schedule your focus group sessions for one and a half to two hours, recognizing that the time period you outline defines the maximum length of your session.
- Schedule your focus group for a time and date convenient to participants. Students may require sessions in the early evening. Faculty may be able to find time between classes.
- Schedule more participants than you need, because it is likely that some will not show up. To get eight to ten participants, schedule at least twelve or thirteen.
- Confirm the session via e-mail and place reminder telephone calls the day before the session.
- Make sure your confirmations and reminders include clear instructions on the location, date, and time of the scheduled focus group. Also, consider sharing your proposed agenda for the session with participants. This let will them to know what to expect at their sessions.

Who will observe your sessions?

The nonverbal behavior of participants can add dimension and nuance to what they say. In addition to the moderator, who will make her or his own observations, an observer is recommended to focus specifically on how participants say things and to capture their nonverbal actions, noting where in the discussion they occurred. Some nonverbal cues can be noticed on video if you tape your sessions, but unless you have an advanced video recording system, you will miss a number of off-camera behaviors. The human observer often serves the additional role of running the audio recording device. The moderator should not focus too much on making observations because her or his chief concern is directing the discussion. However, the moderator should briefly note those behaviors that stand out. The moderator's notes can then be fleshed out in a debriefing after the session with the observer.

How will you capture your data?

The simplest approach and one that is usually quite adequate is to have someone serve as the observer/recorder, as we just touched on above. This individual operates an audio recording device, and also makes observations on the nonverbal behavior of participants. Any simple tape recorder will suffice, but take care to test it in the room where your session will be held. Also, have extra blank tapes and batteries on hand. Video recording can also be used to capture sessions. It works best when it can be done unobtrusively (for example, behind a one-way mirror), but you should tell participants that filming is taking place. Even a visible camera can work because participants quickly become accustomed to its presence.

How will your session be organized?

At first glance, the answer to this question may seem a simple one—the moderator follows the interview guide and the group has a discussion. However, a well-run focus group session is actually more complex. You should provide your participants with an agenda (preferably in writing) for their focus group session. This sets expectations and gives participants a sense of what will happen. Figure 8.2 lists the basic components of a focus group agenda. These agenda items will be discussed at length below in the section on "Conducting The Focus Group."

CONDUCTING THE FOCUS GROUP

Before your focus group session begins, create a final checklist to run through in the hours leading up to the session. See Figure 8.3 for an example of what your checklist might look like.

---

1. Welcome
2. Review agenda
3. State purpose of the session
4. Set ground rules
5. Introductions
6. Discussion
7. Session wrap-up

Figure 8.2. Standard Elements of a Focus Group Agenda.

---

1. Check the room. Make sure the temperature is comfortable and that you have enough chairs.
2. Test your recording equipment. Have blank tapes and a backup power supply on hand.
3. Confirm that your materials are in order: agendas, the question guide, paper for notes, pens.
4. Confirm that your refreshments are in order. If serving warm food, take care to not have it prepared too soon. It is often best to allow participants to eat as soon as they arrive and begin the session as they get comfortable.
5. Have nametags prepared for participants, the moderator, and the observer/recorder.
6. Save the moderator's place at the conference table by placing coat on the chair or some papers on the table. The moderator should sit among the participants, toward the center of the table.

Figure 8.3. Example of a Focus Group Checklist.

The Focus Group Session

A simple approach to describing the process of conducting a focus group session is to discuss the elements of the agenda as listed in Figure 8.2 with the addition of one preliminary step—the arrival of participants. Throughout this discussion we will assume that you are moderating the session yourself.

Participants Arrive: You should be completely prepared at this point. Last minute scrambling as participants arrive will not give them a comfortable feeling. Greet participants as they arrive. Introduce yourself and check them in, giving them a nametag. Let them know where the nearest restrooms are located. Offer them refreshments and ask them to take a seat at the conference table.

Welcome: Begin the session at its scheduled time by offering a formal welcome. Introduce yourself to everyone. Thank participants for their involvement. Introduce your observer/recorder and let participants know they will be recorded. This is probably a good time to start recording the session, as participants can begin interacting almost immediately.

Review the Agenda: Refer to the agenda and summarize it for participants.

State the Purpose of the Session: This is a critical step. Summarize your assessment project for participants. Describe your goals and objectives, and importantly, how you plan to use the results. In other words, let participants know how their involvement will help the library. Also, give participants a chance to ask questions at this point.

Set Ground Rules: It is important to briefly set some rules for the session. Here is a brief list of suggested ground rules:

—The session will run for 90 minutes.
—There are no right or wrong answers.
—Each person's views are important to the library.
—Speak loudly enough so all can hear.
—Allow one person to talk at a time.
—Try to stay focused on the questions under consideration.
—Do not shy away from conflicting viewpoints or disagreement. The purpose of our discussion is to share diverse and varied views.
—Respect the views of others, regardless of how much you disagree.
—Each participant is free to stop at any time.

Although the above ground rules seem heavy-handed as a list, the moderator should take care to maintain a friendly and warm tone when discussing them with participants. As many of these rules are usually recognized as standard principles of civilized discourse, you might position these ground rules as reminders.

Introductions: Now you are ready to begin discussion. Start with an icebreaker to get everyone involved and introduced. You might simply ask students to introduce themselves and to describe their most recent experience in relation to the session's main subject. If, for example, you are exploring student perceptions of newly-developed online information literacy tutorials, you might ask students to introduce themselves and state where they were when they first tried the tutorials: in their dorm room, at the library, in the student union using a wireless laptop, and so on.

Discussion: Begin through your question guide. Here are some basic considerations for conducting your discussion:

—Clearly state each question to the participants and give them time to reflect before asking for responses.
—Be alert for appropriate follow-up questions.
—Strive to involve everyone, with transitions like, "That's interesting. What do you think, [participant's name]?"
—Be alert for digressions and monitor the pace. Do not get bogged down on a single issue. You might consider asking your observer/recorder to watch the time and give you signals when you reach the one-hour mark and so forth. Often if your session goes well, the intensity of interaction may make it difficult for you to gauge the time.
—If required, ask participants to speak up or repeat answers.
—When transitioning from question to question, summarize the discussion of the previous point before moving on or moving on to a follow-up question.
—Avoid talking too much. Sometimes participants will ask you for information about the topic being discussed or for your opinion. Be polite and very brief in your response.
—Avoid the urge to correct erroneous information. You may hear participants make incorrect statements. You should not use focus group time to educate or defend. If you wish, you can make a note to have a private, follow-up conversation with the participant later to provide (or seek) clarification.

Session Wrap Up: Close your session with a final summary. Thank participants for sharing their views. Let them know you will share your final assessment report with them. If you have left over food and refreshments, you might offer these before closing the session. You will also want to remain in the room for a few minutes after your session adjourns, in case participants have questions or concerns.

Right after the Session

As soon as possible after your session concludes, meet with your observer/recorder and hold your own wrap-up session. During this meeting you should do a number of things, some of them practical and others more analytical, as you are really beginning the process of data analysis. Additional notes should be taken throughout this debriefing process to capture the moderator's and observer/recorder's reactions, thoughts, and perceptions.

• Check your audio recording.
• Take a few moments to flesh out notes.
• Compare notes and share observations.
• Discuss nonverbal behaviors.
• Discuss what worked and what did not work.
• Note any themes or opinions that seemed prominent.

TRANSCRIBING THE DATA

The data transcription process for focus groups is very similar to the transcription process for interview data. Refer to the "Transcribing The Data" section of Chapter 7 for this discussion.

ANALYZING THE DATA

Once the transcriptions are complete, you are ready to analyze the data. You will have already gained some ideas about themes in the responses. Further analysis of focus group data is usually done using content analysis, which is a more systematic and objective way of examining this rich data and drawing conclusions which you can then act upon. Refer to Chapter 13 for information about content analysis.

EXAMPLE OF A FOCUS GROUP STUDY

The following section provides an overview of an assessment scenario and the focus group planning and preparation process. A sample focus group interview guide is included in Figure 8.4.

Assessment Scenario

Conduct a focus group with English Composition instructors to discuss the pilot implementation of online information literacy modules for their students. The focus group will seek to:

• Provide a preliminary evaluation of the online information literacy modules.
• Explore the perceptions and attitudes of the instructors.

The focus group results will contribute to the overall assessment of the online information literacy modules, which will include student participation rates and performance scores (as collected online), a student survey administered near the end of the course, and feedback gathered from an open-ended form provided online.

Twelve sections of English Composition II piloted the online modules for a semester. Recognizing the strategic role that English instructors play in the program's success, librarians planned a focus group with the instructors in the pilot sections to discuss their attitudes and perceptions. At the same time, librarians hope that by facilitating an open dialog and listening, they will build trust and collaborative support with the instructors.

Program Description: Online Information Literacy Modules for English Composition

As a strategy to deliver information literacy instruction to a large population of students enrolled in English Composition II, the library designed and developed a series of Flash-based online tutorials made available through the university's online learning system. Instructors assign the online modules to their students, asking them to complete five to ten of the modules. The modules play like movies and provide interactive online instruction, and are followed by a brief online quiz. Upon completing a module and quiz, the student's score is sent to the instructor's e-mail. These scores are also copied to a library account. Students scoring below 70% are asked to repeat the module.

The ten modules focus broadly on the ACRL *Information Literacy Competency Standards for Higher Education* (2000), with emphasis on:

- Defining information needs (Standard One, Performance Indicator 1).
- Effective search design and strategy (Standard Two, Performance Indicators 2 through 5).
- Evaluating information critically (Standard Three, Performance Indicators 2 and 4).
- Teaching information ethics and citation standards (Standard Five, Performance Indicators 2 and 3).

The Focus Group Plan

Focus of Discussion: The discussion will focus on two main lines of inquiry: the usability of the online modules and their perceived impact on student learning.

Interview Guide: See Figure 8.4, Focus Group Interview Guide, below.

Moderator: One of the library's instruction librarians will serve as moderator. She has moderated focus groups before and has good interpersonal skills.

When and Where: The focus group will take place during the week prior to the beginning of the spring semester when most instructors are back on campus. It will be held in the English department reading room. The room has a large conference table that seats fifteen comfortably. It is a bit drafty, but the participants will be very familiar with the setting. As a convenience to participants, the focus group will take place directly following an English Composition instructors' meeting (about 3:00 p.m. on a Tuesday), which takes place in the Reading Room.

Number of Sessions: Because only twelve instructors participated in the pilot program, only one session will be scheduled.

Participants: Ten of twelve instructors who participated in the pilot program have confirmed that they plan to stay after their meeting for our focus group discussion.

Rewards: Coffee, juice, and cookies will be served at the beginning of the focus group. Due to the level of integration of the program into the composition curriculum, participants will likely be highly motivated despite a lack of additional rewards.

Observer/Recorder: A graduate student working for the library instruction department will serve as observer for the session and will also operate the tape recorder.

Recording Device: A standard cassette tape recorder will be used. The moderator and observer/recorder will sit at the center of the conference table at a location central to the discussion.

Session Agenda:

Pre-session

- Check tape recorder.
- Informal welcomes.

- Record who shows up.
- Pass out agendas.
- Offer refreshments.

1. Welcome

- Moderator introduces herself/himself.
- Introduce observer/recorder.
- Thanks participants for attending.
- Begin recording.

2. Review Agenda
3. State Purpose of the Session

- Statement of Purpose: "The purpose of this focus group discussion is to explore how the online modules worked for your students and to discuss your initial impressions and comments on the new program. This focus group discussion will contribute to the overall assessment of this pilot program. In addition, we have the online data of your students' performance, we have survey responses gathered from your students at the end of last semester, and feedback from online forms located within the modules."
- "Does anybody have any questions at this point?"

4. Set Ground Rules
(Because the participants are faculty instructors, a certain level of professional decorum may be assumed. The two rules below will probably suffice, but be prepared to remind participants of other "assumed" rules if problems occur.)

- "This session will last about 90 minutes."
- "Please speak loudly so everybody can hear."

5. Introductions

- Start with question 1 on the Interview Guide.

6. Discussion

- Follow Interview Guide.
- Watch for digressions.
- Be ready with appropriate follow-up questions.
- Summarize discussion before transitioning to next question.

7. Session Wrap-Up

- Wrap up the discussion by summarizing some of the main points of discussion.
- Give them an indication of when a report of the results will be ready.
- Thank them again.

Post-session

- Check tape recorder.
- Moderator and observer/recorder take a few minutes to flesh out their notes.
- Moderator and observer/recorder debrief.

1. (Icebreaker) To get started I'd like to hear some of your general or initial impressions of how the online modules worked for your students and classes. Let's go around the room, introduce ourselves, and share one observation or impression that stood out for you.

2. It might be interesting to share how we each used the modules in our classes. How did you assign the modules in your class? Who wants to go first?

   Potential follow-ups or variations:

   • How many of the ten modules did your class use?
   • Do you feel you assigned too few or too many of the modules?
   • What deadlines did you put in place for completing modules?
   • How did you handle students who failed to complete the modules on time?

Summarize major points before moving on.

3. Here's a question that we've been interested in from the start, and I know in our initial discussions with you, it was a concern of yours also. How did the modules work for your class technically?

   Potential follow-ups or variations:

   • Did the reporting system work for you?
   • Did people have trouble accessing the modules?
   • Did they perform properly?
   • Did you hear complaints?
   • Had you worked with the online learning system before?

Summarize major points before moving on.

4. Switching gears a little bit, let's consider how your students performed. We can share with you that the average quiz score across all your sections was 82%. Were you happy with the scores of your class?

   Potential follow-ups or variations:

   • Did the repeat policy for students scoring below 70% work for you?
   • Were you happy with the content of the quizzes in general?

Summarize major points before moving on.

5. How about evidence of student learning in your classroom and in student work? Did you observe students applying what they learned from the modules?

   Potential follow-ups or variations:

   • How did students perform on their research assignments?
   • Did you have any problems with plagiarism?
   • Did you have students who needed additional instruction beyond the modules?

Summarize major points before moving on.

6. We've already heard a lot of great ideas and observations so far, but as we wrap up our discussion, I'd like to ask if you have any final suggestions or comments that we haven't heard yet today.

Go to Session Wrap-Up on agenda.

Figure 8.4. Example of a Focus Group Interview Guide.

ARE FOCUS GROUPS RIGHT FOR YOU?

Review the following factors when considering focus groups:

 Time

The advantage that usually draws researchers to the focus group is its efficient and economical use of time. While planning a focus group is not to be taken lightly and adequate time should be used to prepare, the entire focus group process usually takes less time than a written survey and is certainly shorter than the process of interviewing eight participants separately. In addition, you get a large amount of information in this short period of time. However, sometimes recruiting and scheduling participants can become very time intensive. Careful planning can help avoid these difficulties, but in larger projects in which many focus group sessions are required, you will not be able to avoid spending a great deal of time on recruiting and scheduling.

 Money

The expenses of focus groups are usually minimal because of the time economies discussed above, but focus groups have a lot of "expense options" that can raise your costs. Do you pay participants for their participation? Do you purchase refreshments and snacks for the focus group? Will you use an outside consultant to moderate and/or analyze your data? Also, do you have free access to recording equipment? Will you hire someone to transcribe your data?

 Level of Assessment

Focus groups work well in assessing at the program level, especially for new and evolving programs, but can also provide insights into the general opinions and attitudes held at the institutional level.

 Assessment Domain

Focus group studies shed light on affective outcomes—what people think and feel, their attitudes, values, and perceptions. Moving beyond one-on-one interviews, focus groups invite participants to examine their responses in comparison to other responses. In this way, we get deeper responses, views are re-informed and revised and new views, perhaps previously suppressed, are more likely to be expressed. Knowledge questions and questions about prior behaviors can be included and they can be helpful in gaining context during focus group sessions, but focus groups are not a strong choice for assessing knowledge or behavior in a systematic way.

Access to Participants

Even more so than interviewing, focus groups present challenges in gaining access to and scheduling participants. Participants must be recruited, either independently or with the help of faculty and staff.

 Level of Faculty Collaboration

Faculty collaboration can only aid your focus group project, but it is not absolutely necessary. However, faculty will likely be very interested in program level assessments and may provide valuable input. And as we mentioned above, they can also help out with recruiting students.

Outside Expertise

Do you need outside expertise? This is a question that requires some consideration. As budget pressures rise, we often pass over the idea of hiring experts, assuming we cannot possibly afford it. However, professional consultants can offer valuable expertise in designing your focus group, moderating it, and in analyzing the data. It may be well worth the expenditure to have your focus groups handled professionally.

A middle way is to find experts within your own academic community. Colleagues in other departments may have experience and expertise in focus group methodology that they would be happy to share. You might even find a point of collaboration to explore together.

Beyond budgetary considerations, you will want to consider the level of your assessment project when deciding if you need a consultant. If you have little experience and are embarking on an important assessment project of great interest to administrators, consultants should be a strong consideration. The use of consultants can strengthen the perceived credibility of your assessment results.

WORKS CITED AND FURTHER READING

Association of College and Research Libraries (ACRL). (2000). *Information literacy competency standards for higher education: Standards, performance indicators, and outcomes.* Retrieved May 23, 2006 from www.ala.org/ala/acrl/acrlstandards/informationliteracycompetency.htm.

Gibbs, A. (1997). Focus groups. *Social Research Update.* Retrieved January 9, 2006 from http://sru.soc.surrey.ac.uk/SRU19.html.

Glitz, B. (1997). The focus group technique in library research: An introduction. *Bulletin of the Medical Library Association, 85*(4), 385–390.

Glitz, B. (1998). *Focus groups for libraries and librarians.* Chicago, IL: American Library Association.

Krueger, R. A. (1994). *Focus groups: A practical guide for applied research* (2nd ed.). Thousand Oaks, CA: Sage.

Krueger, R. A. and Casey, M. A. (2000). *Focus groups: A practical guide for applied research* (3rd ed.). Thousand Oaks, CA: Sage.

Morgan, D. L. (1997). *Focus groups as qualitative research* (2nd ed.). Thousand Oaks, CA: Sage.

Patton, M. Q. (1990). *Qualitative education and research methods.* Newbury Park, CA: Sage.

Shoaf, E. C. (2003). Using a professional moderator in library focus groups. *College and Research Libraries, 64*(2), 124–132.

Tiberius, R. (2001). Making sense and making use of feedback from focus groups. *New Directions for Teaching and Learning, 87*, 63–75.

Von Seggern, M. and Young, N. J. (2003). The focus group method in libraries: Issues relating to process and data analysis. *Reference Services Review, 31*(3), 272–284.

Wilcox Johnson, D. (1996). Focus groups. *The TELL IT! manual: The complete program for evaluating library performance.* Chicago, IL: American Library Association.

Young, V. (1993). Focus on focus groups. *College and Research Libraries News, 7*, 391–394.

9

Knowledge Tests

Indicators:

 Requires some time investment for learning test-making skills and for grading essay items

 Requires little money, unless purchasing a standardized test

 Level of assessment: Classroom, Programmatic, Institutional

 Domain: Cognitive

 Access to participants: Requires medium level of effort

 Must get some buy-in and cooperation from faculty

 No outside expertise needed

Key Characteristics:

Objective items

- Assesses students' recall and understanding of facts and concepts.
- Format is familiar and easy for students to follow.
- Requires skill and creativity to write good test questions.
- Scoring is easy and fast.
- Can be effectively used for pre- and post-testing.

Essay items

- Strong choice to evaluate higher order knowledge and analytic skills.
- Delivers richer information than objective item formats.
- Can be time consuming for students to complete.
- Can be time consuming and difficult to score.

AN OVERVIEW OF KNOWLEDGE TESTS

Knowledge tests focus on what students know, rather than on their skills, behaviors, attitudes, or opinions. With a well-constructed knowledge test, you can find out what facts or concepts students have learned or can recall. Knowledge tests can vary quite a lot in length and still be effective. You can use a very short test of objective items with a one-shot session, or put together a longer and more comprehensive test, including essay questions, for a course. As knowledge tests are a familiar part of academic life, they take very little explanation and students can usually start answering questions right away.

Knowledge tests are well-suited to pre- and post-testing, which is very helpful if you want to measure the effect of your instruction. You can find out how much students learned during your instruction only if you are aware of how much they knew beforehand. However, the time interval between pre- and post-tests is critical. To be effective, pre-testing should be done early enough before the instruction. The post-test given after the session should show some change (we hope it's an increase!) in knowledge over the pretest, but this change can be due to other factors. If a pre-test is given immediately before a one-shot instructional session with the post-test given immediately afterwards, you will be testing short-term memory but probably not longer-term retention or true learning. If too much time passes between the pre- and post-tests, changes may be due to other growth during that time and not related to your instruction session. It is helpful to keep in mind that additional factors may influence students' learning, such as class assignments, events either at the institution or in the world, and students' outside interests. When you see an improvement between pre- and post-tests, you must interpret it cautiously.

Knowledge tests should, of course, be tied closely to the learning objectives and the concepts being taught. The questions on a knowledge test should be taken from the material that was covered during the instruction. Test questions should be written carefully and with attention to how the question might be interpreted by the test-taker.

In this chapter we offer information about and guidelines for writing two different types of knowledge test items, objective test questions and essay questions. Both may be used in a knowledge test, alone or in combination.

Types of Knowledge Test Items

Objective Items

Objective test questions are usually quite short and have one correct answer that is predetermined. From in-class use to final exams to national, standardized tests such as the SAT, objective tests are very common at most educational levels so they are familiar to students. Objective tests continue to be a very popular option for measuring knowledge, despite criticisms over the years. With careful attention to the writing of valid objective test items, this method of testing is an efficient and accurate measure of certain types of knowledge, like remembering, understanding, and perhaps evaluating. In information literacy testing, objective items are used to measure a student's ability to recall facts and to make lower-level cognitive judgments based on the material covered in instruction. Many of the learning objectives in Standards One and Two of the ACRL *Information Literacy Competency Standards for Higher Education* (2000) are suitable for testing with objective items.

Basic terminology used when discussing knowledge tests is presented in Figure 9.1. In the section "Objective Items" below, we will describe four common types of objective items: multiple-choice, true/false, matching, and completion.

Essay Items

Essay items are typically used to measure more subjective and analytical skills. In particular, essay items are useful for information literacy learning objectives that focus on developing students' abilities to plan and organize a research strategy, evaluate information, and synthesize new information into their existing knowledge bases. As essay items can be time consuming for students, you should be selective in choosing which learning objectives to cover with this method.

For many instructors, essay items are easier to write than objectives items. However, although it may be easier to prepare essay items, the time commitment evens out between essay items and objective test items once we start to grade the tests (Tuckman 1993, p. 22).

Test-makers and researchers use a common vocabulary when talking about objective tests:

Item—the test question, which is made up of the <u>stem</u>, the <u>correct choice</u>, and one or more <u>distractors</u>.

Stem—in multiple-choice and matching items, stems are statements that present a problem.

Response options—in multiple-choice and matching items, the possible solutions to the problem presented in the stem. There are two types of response options, the <u>correct choice</u> and <u>distractors</u>.

Correct choice—this is the unambiguously correct answer for the stem.

Distractors—the response options that are incorrect.

Example:

Stem:	If you wanted to search for a topic that has several components, such as nutrition for pregnant women, which operator would you use?
distractor:	a. ADJ
correct choice:	b. AND
distractor:	c. NEAR
distractor:	d. NOT
distractor:	e. OR

Figure 9.1. Knowledge Test Terminology.

The simple mechanics of reading each essay is more time-consuming than grading a multiple-choice test with a key; however, reading is only part of the scoring, as we will see. So, although essay items may save time at the outset, they should be used only when they are the best way to measure objectives.

CREATING KNOWLEDGE TESTS

Knowledge tests such as the SAT and ACT, which carry very high-stakes consequences with them, go through extremely rigorous development processes to ensure fairness and accuracy. You do not need to spend such enormous resources perfecting your test questions, but there are several simple rules to follow to make sure your test items are good ones. Good item planning and writing is essential to avoid four potential pitfalls related to test validity. Validity refers to how well the measurement tool, in this case the knowledge test, measures the phenomenon of interest. In our case, we are interested in measuring knowledge of information literacy constructs. Careless construction of a knowledge test can result in student scores that reflect things other than information literacy ability. Students may score poorly if they are confused about how to complete the test, if they lack advanced reading skills, or if they do not have enough time to answer all the questions. On the other side of the coin, students can end up with artificially high scores if they are savvy test-takers, alert for cues as to which are the correct answers. (One common cue provided by test-makers by mistake: The correct answer in a multiple-choice question is noticeably longer than the incorrect answers.)

Another area to watch is content validity. A knowledge test should cover the instructional material adequately, so that students have an opportunity to show their knowledge in all areas. The test should also avoid covering material that was not included in the instruction.

Objective Items

Four of the most common types of objective items are: multiple-choice, true/false, matching, and completion. You are no doubt familiar with these types of questions from your own academic career. Figure 9.2 presents examples of each question type for an information literacy concept.

There are many helpful guides to making knowledge tests, most of which include several "rules" for writing test items. Frey et al. (2005) examined research studies to find out which rules are supported by experimental results. They identify those few rules that have empirical support (only four!), plus rules that are commonly recommended by experts. Figure 9.3 is taken from Frey et al.'s list and will give you a strong set of guidelines to follow.

Preparing Good Objective Items

It can be a bit daunting to create test items from scratch, but it is a skill that develops quickly once you start. Begin with the instructional material to be covered and decide what is important enough to test. You will need to choose the type of item to use. It is a good idea to keep to as few item types as possible. In other words, if you have a short, 10-item test, do not use two multiple-choice, one true/false, four matching, and three completion items. Try to have at least five of each item type, which in this case means you would only use one or two types of items.

All four examples are based on a learning objective from ACRL's (2001) *Objectives for Information Literacy Instruction: A Model Statement for Academic Librarians.*

Learning objective: The information literate student names the three major disciplines of knowledge (humanities, social sciences, sciences) and some subject fields that comprise each discipline.

Assumption: You have presented instructional material about what the major disciplines are and some subject fields for each.

Multiple-choice item	Which of the following subject fields belongs to the humanities discipline? Choose one answer.
	❏ Biology ❏ Chemistry ❏ Medicine ❏ Philosophy ❏ Sociology

True/False	Mark each item T for true or F for false.
	_____ One of the three major disciplines of knowledge is history.

Matching	Directions: For each subject field in column 1, find the major discipline it belongs to in column 2. Write the letter preceding the discipline in the blank to the left of the subject field.

	Column 1	Column 2
	_____ Biology _____ Chemistry _____ English _____ Geology _____ Music _____ Philosophy _____ Political science	a. Humanities b. Sciences c. Social sciences

Completion	Complete each sentence.
	The three major disciplines of knowledge are _____, _____, and _____.

Figure 9.2. Examples of Types of Objective Items.

This chart offers collective advice from test-makers and researchers for making tests as effective and valid as possible. The first column is the rule or guideline; the other columns show which type of items the guideline applies to.

	Multiple Choice	True/ False	Matching	Completion
*"All of the Above" should not be an answer option.	X			
*The order of the answer options should be logical or vary.	X			
*There should be three to five answer options.	X			
*Complex item formats (for example, "a and b, but not c") should not be used.	X			
"None of the Above" should not be an answer option.	X			
Negative wording should not be used.	X			
Specific determiners (for example, always, never) should not be used.	X			
Stems must be unambiguous and clearly state the problem.	X			
Answer options should not be longer than the stem.	X			
Items should be independent of each other.	X			
Multiple choice stems should be complete sentences.	X			
The correct answer should not be the longer answer option.	X			
All answer options should be plausible.	X		X	
Answer options should include only one correct answer.	X		X	
Answer options should all be grammatically consistent with the stem.	X		X	
Answer options should be homogeneous.	X		X	
Vague frequency terms (for example, often, usually) should not be used.	X	X		
True-false items should have a simple structure.		X		
True-false items should be entirely true or entirely false.		X		

There should be an equal number of true and false statements.		X		
True-false statements should be of equal length.		X		
In matching, there should be more answer options than stems.			X	
Matching item directions should include basis for matching.			X	
In fill-in-the-blank items, a single blank should be used, at the end.				X
Items should cover important concepts and objectives.	X	X	X	X
All parts of an item should appear on the same page.	X	X	X	X
Questions using the same format should be together.	X	X	X	X
Directions should be included.	X	X	X	X
Test copies should be clear and readable (not handwritten).	X	X	X	X

Figure 9.3. Rules for Writing Objective Test Items.

*This guideline is supported by research. Not following this rule will very likely have a negative effect on the validity of your test item.

Source: Frey, B. B., Petersen, S., Edwards, L. M., Pedrotti, J. T., and Peyton, V. (2005). Item-writing rules: Collective wisdom. *Teaching & Teacher Education, 21*(4), 357–364.

In addition to the rules in Figure 9.3, a first-rate guide to writing items is *Developing Classroom Tests* by Kryspin and Feldhusen (1974).

Multiple-choice items: The stem of the item should present a clear and complete question. Try to avoid long stems that challenge students' reading ability. Use simple, direct language. There should be one unambiguously correct answer.

Creating plausible distractors can be the most difficult challenge. You must come up with two to four response options that are incorrect, yet could be selected by a student who does not know the correct answer. Educators sometimes use the distractors to be entertaining. You may remember a test you took that included such distractors: *Question: What is the age of our Sun? Response option a: Not as old as your teacher.* Although these can be amusing, they are not good practice. Having a distractor that is clearly not the correct answer is the same as not having the distractor at all.

You can create distractors by using information that is similar to the correct answer. In the example above, the correct answer was a subject field in the humanities. The other

---

What is the name of a bibliographic management software program that you can use to keep track of your citations?

a. Refworks
b. Reference Works
c. ReferWorks
d. Refwords

Figure 9.4. Example of an Item with Poor Distractors.

True statement:	AND, OR, NOT are examples of Boolean operators.
False statement, poor example:	AND, OR, NOT are examples of Georgian operators.
False statement, better example:	A, AN, THE are examples of Boolean operators.

Figure 9.5. Examples of True and False Statements.

Directions: For each subject field in Column 1, find the major discipline it belongs to in Column 2.

Column 1	Column 2
——— Biology	a. Humanities
——— English	b. Sciences
——— Political science	c. Social Sciences

Figure 9.6. Example of a Poorly Written Matching Item.

distractors were also subject fields, but from other disciplines. You can also get ideas for distractors by anticipating what students could be confused about. Be careful here not to "trick" students by giving the distractors that are too similar to the correct answer or that differ only in trivial ways. Figure 9.4 is an example of an item with distractors that are too similar.

True/false: For these types of items, you must write statements that are clearly and entirely true or not true. Keep the statements simple by including only one idea and cover only important information, not trivia. Writing false statements is more challenging than writing true ones. As with the distractors in multiple-choice items, it is important to avoid tricking the student. Figure 9.5 provides examples of true and false statements.

Matching: Matching items allow for a lot of material to be covered efficiently. The stems and responses should be simple and of the same type. It is good practice to offer more responses than stems so that students do not get items correct simply by narrowing down the options. Write clear directions so students know if they should write the letter of the correct response or draw lines. See Figure 9.6 for an example of an item that does not follow these guidelines and therefore does not give us much useful information.

Completion: Completion items should ask a student to provide key information to make a statement complete and accurate. The part of the statement presented to the student should be well-defined and clear. The answer or answers to be provided should be the only correct answers. In Figure 9.7 you can see how a poorly written completion item can be improved.

Poor Example:	The invisible college is a _____.
	[This is more an example of a restricted-response essay question.]
Poor Example:	The _____ college is a system of _____
	communication that relies on _____ such as discussion lists
	and _____.
Better Example:	A system of scholarly communication that relies on informal interactions
	such as discussion lists and personal contacts is known as _____.
	[Notice that the article "an" is not provided before the blank. This avoids
	giving the clue that the answer starts with a vowel.]

Figure 9.7. Examples of Completion Items.

Reviewing Objective Items

The best practice for reviewing the items is to work with members of your target population (that is, students) who will not be taking the test. Identify and invite students who are at the same level as the students you will be instructing to go over the items with you. Realizing that these students have not received the instruction you will base your testing on, do not expect them to know all the correct answers. However, they can let you know about confusing directions, tricky wording, or unknown terminology. You can decide if revision of the item is necessary.

You can also ask some of these students to simply take the test. Reassure them that you are not testing their knowledge but instead are asking them to test your test. (Students may get discouraged if they find they do not know many correct answers.) This process will give you a good idea of how long it will take students to complete the test so that you can allocate sufficient time.

Presenting the Items

Once you have all your objective items ready, decide how you want to administer the test. Will it be a paper and pencil test? If so, be sure to type the items (no handwriting) and to keep all parts of an item on the same page. Give some thought to how the items will be scored as this will affect your arrangement of items on the page. For example, it will be easier to compare a student's responses on matching items to a key if the student must write the letters of correct responses down the left side of the page.

There are several good software packages available for giving tests. Some offer grading, data tabulation, and even immediate feedback of results to the student. Costs range from nothing for freeware to significant membership charges. Another option may be your university's online learning system, such as Blackboard or WebCT. A good option if you are doing instruction for a faculty member who uses the online learning system is to collaborate with the person to put up a quiz or test on the class site in the online learning system. Figure 9.8 lists some online software programs.

Regardless of format, group similar types of items together and give clear directions for what the student is to do in each section. If the test will not count toward a student's grade, include a statement or two encouraging students to do their best. Briefly explain how the results will be used (for example, to identify gaps in knowledge that will be addressed in future sessions, to design instruction for future classes) and the importance of their active participation.

Hot Potatoes—http://hotpot.uvic.ca/.

"The *Hot Potatoes* suite includes six applications, enabling you to create interactive multiple-choice, short-answer, jumbled-sentence, crossword, matching/ordering and gap-fill exercises for the World Wide Web. Hot Potatoes is not freeware, but it is free of charge for those working for publicly-funded non-profit-making educational institutions, who make their pages available on the web."

Question*mark*—www.questionmark.com.

"The Question*mark*™ Perception™ assessment management system enables educators and trainers to author, schedule, deliver, and report on surveys, quizzes, tests and exams. This complete assessment management system enables you to create questions and organize them into exams, quizzes, tests or surveys. You can schedule people to take the assessments, deliver them in a variety of ways and then view the results in 11 different report types."

Quia Web—www.quia.com.

Quia offers an array of educational games and activities. The service relevant to offering knowledge tests is the ability to create online quizzes using several different item formats. Quizzes are graded immediately with feedback provided to the student. Individual instructors pay a $49 subscription rate; other pricing is available for institutions and groups subscriptions.

Test Pilot—www.clearlearning.com/.

Test Pilot is a tool for creating and delivering assessments online. It can accommodate many different types of questions, including audio and video. Three versions are available.

Figure 9.8. Selected Software Programs for Computerized Testing.

Scoring Objective Items

As you create items, keep a version of each item with the correct answer indicated. Use this to create an answer key that can be compared with students' responses for grading. Be sure to note any variations you will accept as correct (though remember that there should usually be just one correct response). For example, for a question about periodicals, you might decide to accept "periodical," "journal," or "magazine." Note these alternatives on your answer key.

Decide how many points each item is worth. The simplest method, well-suited for objective test items, is to make each answer worth one point. Then determine the maximum number of points possible.

For most knowledge tests, scoring is based on how many items a student answered correctly. You add up the points earned and give students that point total. You can also calculate the percentage of correct responses for each student.

Essay Items

Restricted Response Essay Items

Restricted response items set parameters for the student's response. The length of the essay or the exact content to be discussed is specified in the item itself (Oermann 1999, p. 29).

Examples include essay items that limit the student to one paragraph, or items that require the test-taker to define or discuss one or a select number of concepts. See Figure 9.9 for examples of restricted response items.

These three examples of restricted response essay items are based on the ACRL *Information Literacy Competency Standards for Higher Education* (2000) and demonstrate how easily restricted response items can be written to test well-written learning objectives. However, they also demonstrate the limits of restricted response essay items. All three items are written to measure the extent to which students retain facts covered as part of instruction. Each objective measured by these examples could also be measured by using an objective item. As we will see, scoring even restricted response essay items is more involved than objective items, so restricted response items can be avoided in favor of well-written objective items.

Extended Response Essay Items

Extended response essay items allow students more freedom in their responses. They do not set limits on the length or exact content to be discussed in the student's essay and they allow students to demonstrate more knowledge, critical thinking, and creativity. Examples include items that require students to discuss a strategy, create a plan, or discuss a concept. See Figure 9.10 for examples of extended response items for information literacy concepts.

Extended response essay items are more difficult to score than restricted response items (Oermann 1999, p. 29); however, they offer measurement opportunities not available through other test item options such as restricted response essay items or objective items. This feature makes the student effort and time required to answer them and instructor effort in preparing and scoring them well worthwhile. Extended response items are particularly well-suited for measuring higher-level cognitive skills, which means they are a good option to measure learning objectives that require students to analyze, use, and synthesize information, all of which are higher-level information literacy skills.

Preparing Good Essay Items

As is the case for any knowledge testing, the first step for writing essay items is to select the learning objectives that are to be tested and to write the item based on the objective.

- Discuss the difference between a general and subject-specific information resource. Limit your response to one paragraph.
- Briefly identify the three major disciplines of knowledge and one subject that is included in each.
- Identify three formats in which information is available and discuss the usefulness of each.

Figure 9.9. Examples of Restricted Response Essay Items.

- You are required to write a ten-page paper for your senior seminar. Describe your research strategy.
- How do you determine whether your research topic is too narrow, too broad, or suitable?
- Describe the "invisible college" and its usefulness in conducting research.

Figure 9.10. Examples of Extended Response Essay Items.

Practically speaking, you will get the most out of extended response essay items, so it is best to make sure that the objective that you are measuring requires the student to demonstrate a higher-level information literacy skill or to synthesize complex information. Due to the time commitment that essay items or tests require, it is also necessary to make sure that the objective being tested is an important component of your instruction.

Once you have selected the objective to be tested and have determined that an essay item is the best option, it is important to make sure that the item is clearly written. Even if it is an extended response item, make sure that the item gives students clear direction regarding the content to be discussed. Using terminology and, when applicable, scenarios or examples from the class sessions will also help students to associate the item with the objectives that you are attempting to measure.

The next step is to draft at least an outline of an ideal response to the item, to be used in scoring the item. It is not necessary to write a complete narrative response to the item; however, if you do, it can be useful in estimating how long it will take the student to complete the item. Oermann suggests that you time yourself writing an ideal response in narrative form and multiply that time by two to get an estimate of how long it will take your students to complete the item (1999, p. 30). An outline will suffice for scoring purposes, so you can also estimate how long it would take you to write a response and multiply that estimated time by a factor of two or three (depending upon the level of the course) to approximate your average student's response time (Ornstein, 1992). See Figure 9.11 for an essay item preparation checklist.

Reviewing Essay Items

In order to make sure that each item is clearly written, it is a good idea to have someone read it and give you feedback. Most instructors rely on colleagues, and this can be very useful, but terminology that makes sense to colleagues may not make sense to students. Librarians are lucky in that we can get feedback from the students with whom we work regarding the wording of the essay item. If you have students available to review your items, ask them to read the item and indicate what they think it is asking them to do. Ask for feedback regarding confusing wording, instructions, and how much they think they would write on the topic.

Scoring Essay Items

Complications in scoring essay tests and items are clearly the biggest disadvantages in using them for assessment. Scoring essay items is time consuming and invites subjectivity, which can make essay items less reliable measures than objective items.

—— Item assesses a higher order learning outcome.

—— Item is clearly written.

—— Instructions are included and clearly written.

—— At least an outline of a correct response is written for scoring purposes.

—— Essay items and the test as a whole have been checked to make sure that students can complete the test in a reasonable amount of time.

Figure 9.11. Essay Item Preparation Checklist.

Although it is nearly impossible to make scoring essay items less time consuming, there are techniques you can use to make the scoring more objective and reliable. Before we look at how to make scoring less subjective, it is important to identify factors that affect objectivity when scoring essay items:

- Student response patterns
- Student reputation
- Student performance on the test
- Handwriting and grammar

It is easy to be unduly influenced by the structure or tone of student responses to your essay items when scoring. Students may miss the point of the item, but write a well organized, plausible essay, which may invite a good score. Although these essays may demonstrate the student's writing and reasoning abilities, they do not demonstrate the skills that the item is designed to measure. In order to avoid being influenced by these responses, it is important to know what you are looking for when scoring the essay items, which can be accomplished by outlining an ideal response to your item. Once you have written the outline, mark those elements of the outline that you consider to be essential to a good response. It is important that the weighted outline be written, to avoid the tendency to be won over by student essays that are off the mark (Coker et al. 1988, p. 255). Assign a point value to each essential element and a point value to all of the less essential elements combined. For example, if you have three essential elements and there are another five that could be included, you can assign one point for each essential element and another two points for the other elements, making the item worth five points. It is not necessary to assign the same point values for each essay item, nor is it necessary to make the point value a round number like five. Using the outlining method makes it unnecessary to construct a detailed scoring rubric for each essay item, which can be extremely time consuming. For more information on rubrics, see Chapter 11.

A student's reputation can also influence your reading of the essay. This is more of a problem in a stand-alone information literacy course, or in a course-integrated situation in which you get to know the students very well. When you find yourself in a situation where you know students by name, it is important to keep the grading anonymous. If you are scoring the essay portion of a mixed format test, turn to the essay section in each paper, shuffle the papers, and begin your scoring, being careful not to look at the name on the first sheet of the test.

The student's reputation and performance on the other test items can also influence your scoring. In order to ensure that you are scoring only the student's response to the item itself, it is a good idea to score each essay independently. For example, score the first essay item on each exam first and then move onto the second item once the first essays are all scored. To maintain student anonymity, shuffle the papers again once you have finished grading each student's response to the essay item. Cover the student's response to the earlier essay items to keep the score or notes that you wrote from influencing your scoring.

Extraneous factors such as a student's handwriting, diction, and grammar can also influence your scoring if you let them. Unless those skills are being measured by the essay item, which should never be the case for any information literacy assessment, you should try to ignore them. The best advice is to at least be conscious of the effect that the essay's mechanics can have on your scoring so that you can avoid or at least reduce their influence. See Figure 9.12 for the essay item scoring checklist.

—— Correct response outlined.

—— Point values assigned for essential elements of a correct response.

—— Point values assigned for all other elements combined.

—— Tests shuffled and student names covered.

—— Each essay item scored individually.

—— Tests shuffled after each essay item is scored.

Figure 9.12. Essay Item Scoring Checklist.

STANDARDIZED TESTS

You may wish to consider using one of the ready-made standardized information literacy tests that have become available in the past few years. Three tests have come to prominence and are available for purchase. All three build on the ACRL *Information Literacy Competency Standards for Higher Education* (2000). As they have widely varying testing methods, assumptions, report options, and pricing models, you should consult the individual Web sites for details and the most up-to-date information.

iSkills, formerly ICT Literacy Assessment, is a comprehensive test of information and communication technology proficiency from the Educational Testing Service (ETS). It uses scenario-based tasks to measure both cognitive and technical skills covering seven proficiencies which are based in part on the ACRL Information Literacy Competency Standards for Higher Education. The assessment provides support for institutional ICT literacy initiatives, guides curricula innovations, informs articulation and progress standings, and assesses individual student proficiency. More information may be found on the ETS Web site (http://www.ets.org/iSkills).

Information Literacy Test (ILT) is a computerized, multiple-choice test developed collaboratively by the James Madison University Center for Assessment and Research Studies (CARS) and JMU Libraries. It is designed to assess the ACRL Information Literacy Competency Standards for Higher Education. The ILT may be used for program assessment or to test the competency of individual students. More information may be found at the JMU Institute for Computer-Based Assessment Web site (www.jmu.edu/icba/prodserv/instruments_ilt.htm).

Standardized Assessment of Information Literacy Skills (Project SAILS) is a test of information literacy skills based on objectives and outcomes that make up the ACRL Information Literacy Competency Standards for Higher Education. With initial funding from the Institute of Museum and Library Services and 80 participating institutions, the test was developed and is maintained at Kent State University in Ohio. The test allows libraries to document information literacy skill levels for groups of students, to compare results with other schools, and to target areas for improvement. SAILS is a knowledge test with multiple-choice questions targeting eight information literacy skill sets. It can be administered on the Web or on paper. For more information go to www.projectsails.org.

ANALYZING THE DATA

One of the most important steps you can take with data from knowledge tests is to provide feedback to the students who took the test or wrote the essays. Letting the students know how they did is very important for student learning. In this way, knowledge testing serves two purposes: It is a useful tool for assessing instruction, and it is also a tool for student learning.

For objective test items, you should return the scored tests to the students, indicating which items they got correct and which were incorrect (and letting them know the correct response). For essay items, as you read and score each item, make notes of good and bad aspects of the student's response. Be sure to make substantive notes. Simply writing "good" is unlikely to offer the student anything constructive. Comments such as "good analysis of the topic" or "this aspect of your essay should be more developed" are more useful to the student's learning, and help to explain the score that they received on the item.

You can do further work with the scores on knowledge tests. For objective tests, once you have scored all students on all items, you can create a simple frequency distribution to provide a summary of the class overall. Order score values from highest to lowest and enter the number of times each score occurred. This will show you the range of scores obtained as well as the more frequently-occurring ones. In addition to giving you a snapshot of how the class did, it is useful to your students to see where their scores are in relation to the rest of the class.

Another way to examine the data is to note how many responded correctly to each item. If there are items that many students missed there are two possible explanations. One is that the information was not adequately covered in your instruction. Another is that the item is not well written. If the content was indeed presented, you should read the item and any response options carefully to see if you spot any problems with the item.

You should also use the information gathered through knowledge tests to review your instructional techniques. Questions that were missed by many students can give you a quick guide for targeting improvements to your instruction. You will have to decide for yourself how many students have to miss a question for it to merit your attention. Look at the combination of the importance of the concept and the number of students who missed it to prioritize where you will devote the most effort.

ARE KNOWLEDGE TESTS RIGHT FOR YOU?

Review the following factors when considering knowledge tests:

 Time

Knowledge test items require careful attention to content and construction of the items. The total amount of time needed for knowledge tests depends in large part on how comprehensive you want the test to be. If you want to test students' knowledge after weeks of instruction, then clearly you will need to devote considerable time to creating items that cover that material. If you want to add a few test items to a faculty member's exam, it will take less time, though you should still be careful to write good items and review them. As mentioned above, scoring of essay items requires significant time.

 Money

Knowledge tests require no outside funds, unless you choose to use online software to administer a test that you developed. Even then, there are free software options available. Another potential source of cost is purchasing a standardized test, mentioned previously in this chapter.

 Level of Assessment

Knowledge testing is appropriate for all three levels of assessment. Objective items in particular can be used with one-shot instruction. Essay items are a good choice for longer-term instruction over a course or a set of courses. Administering knowledge tests for institutional assessment can give you a good snapshot of students' level of knowledge, which may compare to test results at a later date. Or you may compare one group of students with another (for example, freshmen and juniors, or family studies majors and English majors). Some standardized tests also allow comparison with other institutions.

 Assessment Domain

Assessing students' knowledge reveals information about their cognitive skills or judgments. Keep in mind that actual student behavior can be quite different from what students demonstrate in a knowledge test. Also, students' attitudes and feelings affect the choices they make in seeking information. You should consider rounding out your assessment with behavioral and affective assessments.

 Access to Participants

If you give some knowledge test items during a one-shot instructional session, you already have access to the students. More comprehensive testing, including longer tests, using essay items, and pre- and post-testing, requires working with faculty, as described below.

 Level of Faculty Collaboration

Knowledge testing is almost always tied to a particular instructional effort, whether a lesson, a module, an entire course, or a program of courses. Unless you are teaching the course yourself, you will need to work closely with the classroom faculty. You may need to seek time in their classes for pre- or post-testing, or their permission and cooperation to add test items to their exams or their online learning course sites. In any case, faculty support and buy-in is essential; faculty can make a big difference in how seriously students approach the test, even if the test is not graded.

 Outside Expertise

You will be able to develop the skills needed to write, review, administer, grade, and analyze test items yourself.

WORKS CITED AND FURTHER READING

Angelo, T. A. and Cross, K. (1993). *Classroom assessment techniques: A handbook for college teachers* (2nd ed.). San Francisco, CA: Jossey-Bass Publishers.

Association of College and Research Libraries (ACRL). (2000). *Information literacy competency standards for higher education: Standards, performance indicators, and outcomes.* Retrieved June 16, 2006 from www.ala.org/ala/acrl/acrlstandards/informationliteracycompetency.htm.

Association of College and Research Libraries (ACRL). (2001). *Objectives for information literacy instruction: A model statement for academic librarians.* Retrieved May 23, 2006 from www.ala.org/ala/acrl/acrlstandards/objectivesinformation.htm.

Coker, D. R., Kolstad, R. K., and Sosa, A. H. (1988). Improving essay tests: Structuring the items and scoring responses. *The Clearing House, 61*, 253–255.

Criswell, J. R. and Criswell, S. J. (2004). Asking essay questions: Answering contemporary needs. *Education, 124*(3), 510–516.

Frey, B. B., Petersen, S., Edwards, L. M., Pedrotti, J. T., and Peyton, V. (2005). Item-writing rules: Collective wisdom. *Teaching & Teacher Education, 21*(4), 357–364.

Haladyna, T. (2004). *Developing and validating multiple-choice test items.* Mahwah, NJ: Lawrence Erlbaum.

Kryspin, W. J. and Feldhusen, J. F. (1974). *Developing classroom tests: A guide for writing and evaluating test items.* Minneapolis, MN: Burgess Pub. Co.

Nitko, A. J. (2001). *Educational assessment of students* (3rd ed.). Upper Saddle River, NJ: Merrill.

Oermann, M. H. (1999). Developing and scoring essay tests. *Nurse Educator, 24*(2), 29–32.

Ornstein, A. C. (1992). Essay tests: Use, development, and grading. *The Clearing House, 65*, 175–177.

Tuckman, B. W. (1993). The essay test: A look at the advantages and disadvantages. *NASSP Bulletin, 77*, 20–26.

10

Concept Maps

Indicators:

 Requires a significant time commitment

 Requires little or no money

 Level of assessment: Classroom

 Domain: Cognitive

 Access to participants: Requires medium level of effort

 Ranges from little need for faculty collaboration to some cooperation needed

 No outside expertise needed

Key Characteristics:

- Provides a graphic representation of the ways in which people organize knowledge.
- Demonstrates the ways in which students integrate new information into their knowledge bases.
- Consists of concepts and the relationships among them.
- Allows the instructor to see the ways in which students misunderstand instructional content.
- Can be used for both instruction and assessment of learning.
- Good for pre- and post-testing in extended instruction.
- Can be time consuming.

AN OVERVIEW OF CONCEPT MAPS

Concept mapping is a powerful tool for both instruction and assessment of learning in the classroom. Concept maps offer unique opportunities to help students integrate new concepts into their existing understanding of information seeking, evaluation, and use, and to allow the instructor to gauge that understanding. Concept maps have been used as a tool for instruction and evaluation for more than twenty years, most prominently in the science classroom and more recently across other disciplines, including information literacy instruction. As we will see, some learning outcomes associated with information literacy make concept mapping a good assessment option.

Concept maps are graphic representations of the ways that people organize their knowledge. They depict concepts and the relationships among them that shape perception (Beyerbach 1986, p. 2). Concept maps are made up of nodes representing concepts and labeled lines connecting them, which indicate the relationship between those concepts. The most basic concept map has two concepts and one relationship between them (Novak and Gowin 1984, p. 15).

Concept maps are commonly used to assess the success of any type of instruction at integrating new concepts into a student's understanding. In this use, they provide an illustration of what was learned (Novak and Gowin 1984, p. 15) as well as what was not fully integrated or understood. Although other assessment techniques allow you to identify problem areas, concept mapping is unique in that it can show how the new concepts were not integrated. Reviewing concept maps for an entire class can reveal patterns of misconception among students, which can help to clarify your approach in future instructional situations or sessions.

Concept maps can be used for assessment in any type of information literacy instruction. They are best used to evaluate the effectiveness of information literacy instruction focusing on concepts such as research strategy, publication cycle, types of information resources for specific disciplines, and evaluation of information resources for authority and applicability to a research topic. If we look to the ACRL *Information Literacy Competency Standards for Higher Education* (2000), instruction that focuses on competency Standard Three ("The information literate student evaluates information and its sources critically and incorporates selected information into his or her knowledge base and value system") could appropriately be measured using concept maps.

Concept maps are used much more often in long-term instruction than one-shot sessions. There are three reasons for this. First, concept mapping is time intensive and may be new to students. The resulting learning curve can use up a lot of precious time in a one-shot session. Second, concept maps are ideally used as a pre-test and post-test for students and therefore work best in assessing course-integrated information literacy instruction and stand-alone information literacy courses. Third, when concept maps are used in one-shot sessions, they are typically used for instruction, not for assessment. However, if you want to try it out, you can have students create concept maps toward the end of a session, particularly if the learning objectives of the session focus on clearly distinct skills such as defining a topic or evaluating information resources.

As a librarian, you are most likely to use concept maps in the context of teaching the information literacy portion of a "non-library" course or teaching a stand-alone information literacy course.

TYPES OF CONCEPT MAPS

There are two types of concept maps, hierarchical and flat. Hierarchical maps reflect a discipline's inherent organizational structure, for example, the scientific classification system used to categorize organisms. Hierarchies imply rank or dependent relationships. Flat maps, on the other hand, show relationships that are not based on rank or order. Instead, the relationships show process or equal associations with other concepts.

Hierarchical Concept Maps

Concept mapping was first used by Novak and Gowin (1984) as part of instruction in the sciences. The earliest concept maps reflected the science disciplines and were therefore arranged hierarchically, which means that concepts and relationships move from the top down. See Figure 10.1 for a hierarchically arranged concept map for information literacy.

Flat Concept Maps

As they have been applied to other disciplines, concept maps have expanded to include non-hierarchical or flat arrangements. These are more appropriate when the concepts being studied do not have an intrinsic hierarchy, which is true of many information literacy skills and concepts. In some ways, information literacy is unlike a discipline such as mathematics, where the understanding of basic concepts (for example, arithmetic) lays the foundation for more advanced concepts (for example, algebra). In contrast, understanding how to use Boolean operators is not a prerequisite for understanding other search strategies such as material-type and date limiters.

The decision regarding whether to require a hierarchical arrangement in your concept maps will depend on your instructional objectives. Instruction focusing on

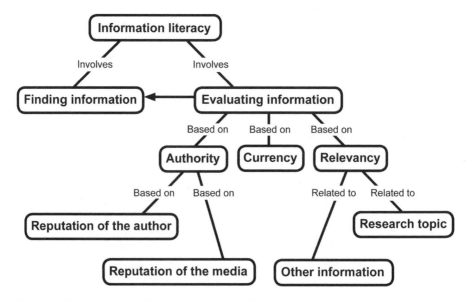

Figure 10.1. Example of a Hierarchical Concept Map.

process-oriented information literacy skills are more suited to flat concept maps. These process-oriented maps may look like flow charts, as in Figure 10.2, below.

CREATING AND USING CONCEPT MAPS

Because concept mapping may be new to many of your students, it is very helpful to orient them to the exercise with an example. If you decide to use concept maps as an assessment tool, it is a good idea to use them in your instruction as well so that students become familiar with them. However, it is better not to use a concept map for teaching the same concept that you will be assessing—students will be required to merely memorize your instructional concept map. You can create a concept map related to one aspect of information literacy on your own and use it in instruction early in the course. For example, you could create a map of the publication cycle and use it as part of your instruction to not only help students understand the publication cycle, but to orient them to concept mapping.

Another option is to create a concept map as a group or class exercise during your instruction. This allows you to not only orient them to concept mapping, but to get an idea of how students understand the concepts to be covered in the course. It is also a good active learning activity. The group or class exercise can serve as a pre-assessment, which can be compared with a similar group or individual concept mapping exercise at the end of the course or instructional sessions.

The process for creating a concept map is the same whether you are doing it on your own or having students create one. Using the evaluation of resources as an example, consider the following scenario. You are teaching the information literacy portion of a freshman composition class and focusing your instruction on evaluating resources based on accuracy, authority, timeliness, and appropriateness of media. You could plan to have the class create a concept map of one aspect of evaluating resources. Start by having the students brainstorm a list of elements to consider when evaluating the author's credibility. The list could include the following:

- Author
- Authority
- Educational background
- Professional experience
- Publications
- Conference presentations
- Awards

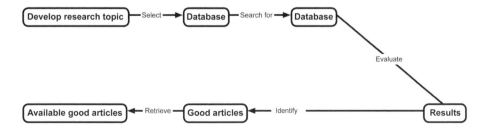

Figure 10.2. Example of a Flat Concept Map.

Once your students have a good list of concepts, write each on a large sticky note. As a class, arrange the sticky notes on a white board to depict the ways in which the concepts are related. Again, it is very important to provide an example of a concept map so that students will understand what they are striving for. Ask the students to decide where to start. In our example, we will start with the concept of the author. Place the "author" sticky note on a whiteboard and ask the students how the author relates to the other concepts on your list. In this case, the author and more specifically, the author's authority, is evaluated based on the other concepts listed. As you move through the list, arrange the concepts on the whiteboard to the class's satisfaction and draw lines between the concepts. At the same time, ask the students how the two concepts are associated. In our example, the "author" is judged by her or his authority, which is determined by the other concepts in our list. Arrange the "authority" sticky note under the "author" sticky note. As they are related, you would then draw a line between the two notes, which depicts the association between the two. As a class or group, discuss the relationship and label it accordingly.

The depth of the group or class exercise depends on how you will use it. If you are using it to familiarize students with concept mapping, you will not need to work through an exhaustive list of concepts. If you are using it as a pre-assessment, more thorough brainstorming and concept mapping may be necessary. If you do want to use concept maps as a pre- and post-test, it is best to do so in small groups or as an individual assignment after having completed or reviewed an example in class.

The process is the same for an individual or small group exercise. Have students start by brainstorming the concepts to be mapped. Each concept will still need a sticky note (albeit a smaller one). For the arrangement of the concepts by small groups or individual students, you will need to provide the students a large sheet of paper and pencils at their desks, and have them arrange the sticky notes on the sheet. Once they are arranged to the students' satisfaction, have them draw the lines between the sticky notes to depict relationships between the concepts labeled on the notes. Each line should then be labeled with the nature of the relationship. See Figure 10.3 for a simple concept map based on this discussion.

Figure 10.3. Example of a Simple Concept Map of Evaluating Sources.

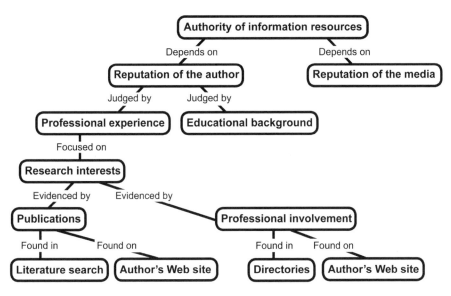

Figure 10.4. Example of a More Fully Developed Concept Map of Evaluating Sources.

Software for concept mapping can make extended evaluation of student learning easier. Freeware options exist that allow you to install the software in your instruction or computing lab for in-class use. Because there is no cost involved, you can reasonably require students to download and install freeware concept mapping software for out-of-class assignments. One of the easiest to use among the freeware options is the CMAP Tools software, available online at http://cmap.ihmc.us/.

Regardless of the format (print or electronic), you may wish to keep copies of the concept maps. If you are starting with a group or class exercise, transcribe the white-board so that you can compare early maps with the maps created at the end of the course or instruction. Taking a digital photo of the whiteboard works well. If you are starting with a group or individual exercise, collect the maps and make photocopies for yourself and the students. Hand the originals back to the students and let them know that they will be doing the same exercise later in the course, so that after the first session they can make notes on their maps as you cover more concepts. If you are using concept mapping software, have the students save their maps and print at least one copy for you to retain. It is also a good idea for them to have a printout to take notes on throughout the course.

At the conclusion of the course or instructional unit, repeat the exercise. You can allow students to use the notes that they have been taking throughout the course. Concept maps are less of a measure of how students recall information than a gauge of how they organize information into their existing knowledge bases, so allowing students to use their notes when completing the later exercise is advisable. See Figure 10.4 for a more fully developed example of a concept map depicting the concepts and relationships in evaluating information sources.

EVALUATING CONCEPT MAPS

Concept maps can be easily evaluated by scoring them. Start by creating an ideal concept map that will serve as an example to use for scoring. To score the example, decide how

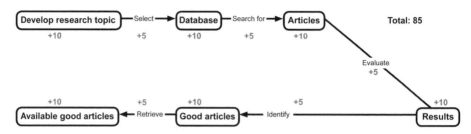

Figure 10.5. Example of an Ideal, Scored Flat Concept Map.

many points to assign to concepts and how many to relationships. Typically, each concept is assigned the same number of points, which is more than the relationships. Relationship points should also be the same for all relationships. For example, the ideal concept map might have six specific concepts at 10 points apiece, and five relationships at five points apiece. That makes the maximum score 85.

When grading a student's concept map, give 10 points for each desired concept, ignoring any concepts that the student included that are not what you are looking for. Give five points for each desired relationship. This part can be a bit tricky because the student may not use the exact wording that you had in mind. Look for conceptual agreement, not language agreement, in order to award the points. In fact, you may decide that the relationships are not crucial and therefore give them no point value at all. See Figure 10.5 for an example of an ideal, scored flat map.

The scored maps can be used to assess the learning that takes place for individual students and the class. Once each map is scored, tabulating the points that were assigned for each element will give you an idea of how many concepts were learned by the average student in your class and how well your students understood how those concepts are related to each other. One benefit to using concept mapping is that you can identify an area that students may not be fully integrating by looking for patterns in the scoring and then in the content of the maps. For example, although instruction focusing on evaluating sources may emphasize six different elements to consider, a review of student concept maps may indicate that typically, only four concepts were included. You could then review the content of your students' maps to see whether it was the same one or two concepts that were consistently left out. If so, you can follow-up with clarification about the missing concepts.

In extended instruction, scoring is useful in both the pre- and post-test phase. If you are assigning a grade or a portion of a grade based on the concept maps created throughout the course, the degree to which the student improved would be the most useful measure of student achievement in the course. A comparison of the scores for early and later concept maps, and not a comparison of scores among students, would be the most useful way to assign grades or evaluate students' conceptual growth throughout the course.

IS CONCEPT MAPPING RIGHT FOR YOU?

Review the following factors when considering concept mapping:

 **Time**

Concept mapping is time consuming, both in its preparation and in its classroom implementation. Although concept maps are increasingly used in other disciplines, students may still be unfamiliar with constructing them, so you will need to plan for careful instructions. The exercise itself is also time consuming. Students will be first compiling a list of the concepts that you presented in your instruction and then creating relationships among them before even mapping anything. If you are using software, the process will not take as much time. Plan on a good portion of a class period regardless of the format you choose.

 Money

Money is not really a factor. If your students are making their concept maps by hand, you will need only regular office supplies: paper, markers, and sticky notes. You may also want to have a large flip-chart and markers. It can be helpful for your students if you present them with a concept map or walk through the process when giving instructions. If you prefer to have your students create electronic concept maps, good and easy-to-use software is available for download at http://cmap.ihmc.us/.

 Level of Assessment

Concept maps are best used in assessing long-term information literacy instruction (for example, course-integrated instruction and stand-alone information literacy courses). They take too much time to realistically use in one-shot instruction. Long-term instruction also takes advantage of a key benefit of concept maps: pre- and post-assessment.

 Assessment Domain

Concept maps are used to assess cognitive outcomes—what students learned as a result of your instructional sessions. Concept maps allow students to demonstrate which new concepts they acquired and how appropriately they integrated those concepts into their existing knowledge bases. Concept maps also identify the concepts that are difficult for students to integrate and show how students perceived the difficult concepts in relation to other concepts that make up their understanding of the content.

 Access to Participants

Because concept maps are best used to assess learning outcomes in a particular course, access to participants will be limited to the students enrolled in that course. You will not be able to effectively use concept maps outside of the classroom.

 Level of Faculty Collaboration

The level of faculty collaboration will depend on your instructional situation. For course-integrated instruction, you will need to request from the faculty member a significant amount of time to do even one concept mapping exercise. Obviously, a pre- and post-test use of concept maps will require more time. Other than the time commitments, you will not need much more from your faculty partner(s) unless you want to do any type of comparison between concept map scores and improvement on other course-related exercises or knowledge tests.

 Outside Expertise

Concept maps are relatively easy to create and evaluate, so outside expertise will not be necessary.

WORKS CITED AND FURTHER READING

Beyerbach, B. A. (1986). *Concept mapping in assessing prospective teachers' concept development.* ERIC Document Reproduction Service No. ED 291800.

Gordon, C. A. (2002). Methods for measuring the influence of concept mapping on student information literacy. *School Library Media Research, 5.*

Jonassen, D. H., Reeves, T. C., Hong, N., Harvey, D., and Peters, K. (1997). Concept mapping as cognitive learning and assessment tools. *Journal of Interactive Learning Research, 8*(3–4), 289–308.

Novak, J. D. (1995). Concept mapping: A strategy for organizing knowledge. In S. M. Glynn and R. Duit (Eds.), *Learning science in the schools: Research reforming practice.* Mahwah, NJ: Lawrence Erlbaum Associates.

Novak, J. D. and Gowin, D. B. (1984). *Learning how to learn.* Cambridge: Cambridge University Press.

Sherratt, C. S. and Schlabach, M. L. (1990). The applications of concept mapping in reference and information services. *RQ, 30,* 60–68.

11

Performance Assessments

Indicators:

 Requires a significant time commitment

$ Requires little money

 Level of assessment: Classroom, Programmatic

 Domain: Behavioral

 Access to participants: Requires medium level of effort

 Requires intense collaboration with faculty

 No outside expertise needed

Key Characteristics of Performance Assessments:

- Focuses on what students can do, especially in regard to real-world problems, like report writing, proposal development, and job searching.
- Strong choice for assessing higher-order thinking skills such as planning, evaluation, interpretation, and navigating complexity.
- Can be used to assess both groups and individuals.
- Often gives students a choice in how they complete their assignments, which can increase motivation and engagement.
- Strong choice for assessing activities and projects, especially those that develop over days, weeks, or months.

- Scoring guides and assignment prompts provide a high level of transparency to people outside of the library.
- Results can offer a high degree of face validity, making them powerful and easily understood by multiple audiences from students to administrators.

AN OVERVIEW OF PERFORMANCE ASSESSMENTS

Performance assessments allow students to demonstrate what they can do, as opposed to describing what they know. They provide a powerful view of how students apply information literacy skills. In working with the ACRL *Information Literacy Competency Standards for Higher Education* (2000), performance assessments may be useful in assessing outcomes that focus on higher order thinking skills, which are associated with various learning outcomes throughout the standards. Higher order thinking skills stress interpretation, synthesis, and planning, so it follows that performance assessments should focus on outcomes that begin with words such as: *develops*, *modifies*, *differentiates*, *implements*, *creates*, *integrates*, *draws conclusions*, and *assesses*.

Performance assessments are sometimes referred to as alternative assessments because they offer an alternative to more traditional knowledge tests. They are used to evaluate student performance by either observation or documentation of the <u>process</u> (for example, executing a search strategy or keeping a research journal) or assessment of a final <u>product</u> (for example, bibliographies, reports, and papers). Figure 11.1 lists some possible performance-based assessments.

Process

Observing a student's performance as he or she executes a task can help you understand the process of how information literacy skills are applied. It allows you to get a direct sense of barriers to student success or new insights as to the pathways students take in retrieving information. This scan of student activity provides you with formative assessment data. One of the disadvantages, however, is that observation of behavior is a time-intensive undertaking. Unless you have extra assistance (colleagues or graduate assistants) it is often not feasible to assess an entire class in this way because you can usually observe only one student at a time.

- Bibliographies
- Essays
- Evaluation reports
- Portfolios (see Chapter 12)
- Presentations
- Research journals
- Research reports
- Speeches
- Student self reflections
- Study guides (student produced)
- Term papers
- Web sites (student produced)

Figure 11.1. Opportunities for Performance Assessments: Sample Assignments.

One option if you have limited resources is to observe a sample of students. Another alternative is to have students do presentations on how they performed a task. Students could be asked to work in small groups to develop a search strategy in a database and then to choose three research articles from the results list. Their presentation to the class might cover the actual decision-making process they used when searching for the articles, as well as the rationale behind their choice of articles. As mentioned above, you can also assess whether students understand a process by requiring written documentation such as a research journal or the submission of a search history from a database. Figure 11.2 offers tips for observing student activities.

Products

As a general rule, assessing the products of student performance is easier and more familiar for most instructors than evaluating a process. After all, research papers have been a staple of college courses for decades. If you are teaching a semester-long class you will have many opportunities for assessing products. If you regularly teach "one-shot" sessions, however, you may wonder how product assessment applies to your situation. Naturally, students won't be turning in an annotated bibliography after a fifty-minute instruction session, but you can work with faculty to assess assignments that are related to the instruction you provide. You might offer to evaluate the citation list for a research paper or to compare students' bibliography annotations to database abstracts. Not only will you gain useful information about students' use of resources, you will also expand your opportunities for collaboration with classroom faculty. You might even want to think about comparing a few papers from a class in which you have done instruction and a few from a class in which you haven't.

Regardless of whether you are assessing a process or product, performance assessments have two components: the assignment and the scoring guide (Suskie 2004, p. 102). The assignment tells students what is expected of them and defines the task they are to complete. The scoring guide is used by the instructor or researcher to evaluate students' performance or end products. Both should relate directly to the skills covered by your learning objectives. Assignments and scoring guides will be covered in this next section.

ASSIGNMENT DESIGN

Although in many cases you will be assisting in the assessment of an assignment designed by someone else, there may be times when you will be designing an assignment

---

- Try to create as natural an environment as possible.
- Include written as well as oral instructions for what you want the students to do.
- Set restrictions, including a time limit.
- To keep things natural, once the assessment begins, answer only questions regarding the instructions.
- Keep students on track by referring to the instructions if you notice that an assignment requirement is being skipped or missed.
- Refrain from correcting or offering suggestions. You are an observer.
- For hands-on activities, include a second scorer if possible.
- Allow students to offer feedback on the assignment or their performance at the conclusion.

Figure 11.2. Guidelines for Observing Student Activities.

from scratch. Here are some tips and guidelines that will help you create effective assignments.

Writing an Assignment Prompt

Developing effective assignments begins with writing the assignment prompt. Prompts are usually written statements that instruct students about what they are to do (Suskie 2004, p. 152). You can either write a <u>restricted prompt</u> or an <u>unrestricted prompt</u>. The type of prompt may be determined by the outcomes that the assignment is designed to assess. For example, an assignment written to assess students' knowledge of Web site evaluation may use a restricted prompt, limiting students to the evaluation of five Web sites and/or requiring them to follow a defined set of evaluation criteria. On the other hand, an assignment designed to assess students' ability to demonstrate <u>how</u> they evaluate those sites in their own research may use an unrestricted prompt asking them simply to research a topic and describe their evaluation process. It is easiest to use restricted prompts whenever you can so that you do not have too many different kinds of responses. So, if your objectives can be assessed by either, we recommend using restricted prompts.

Good performance assignments should allow students to effectively demonstrate the skills being assessed in a reasonable amount of time and with a reasonable amount of effort. For example, annotated bibliography assignments are commonly used to assess students' ability to identify, evaluate, and present information as part of their research process. An annotated bibliography assignment will likely accomplish the same goals by requiring ten citations as it would by requiring twenty. Keeping the assignment reasonable reduces the time students spend completing it as well as the time you spend scoring it.

The assignment prompt should include some introductory text (no more than a sentence or two) to give students the context in which they will be performing the task and to help guide them into the requirements of the assignment. You can use examples from class discussion to help jog their memories as students begin the assignment.

The instructions should also help to focus students on exactly what the assignment is trying to accomplish. Instructions should be clear and direct. You can underline or make bold key words in the instructions to make them clearer for students. In addition to providing the instructions for the assignment, the prompt should provide guidance on how students can meet the requirements. Including a checklist of the required elements of the assignment is helpful. See Figure 11.3 for an example of a restricted prompt for a course assignment in a family studies class.

One Last Check of Your Assignment

Even with all of this in mind, your assignment may not be as clear to your students as it is to you. Before using it for the first time, get some outside feedback on the assignment. One way of doing this is to ask a student to read the assignment and then ask for his or her overall impression. Is it clear? Does it make sense? Are there any words or instructions with which the student is unfamiliar? Once you have a general sense of the clarity of the instructions, ask the student to describe what he or she would do to complete the assignment. If the scenario that your student describes is in line with your expectations and would meet the objectives of the assignment, you are ready to begin.

Family Studies

Library Resources Assignment

Both parts of this assignment are designed to give you an opportunity to practice using University Library resources. Becoming familiar with these resources will assist you as you proceed with coursework in your major. Knowledge of these resources will also aid you in the workplace.

Part I: Locating Professional Journal Articles in Family Studies

Using what you have learned in class about locating library resources, find three journal articles on your selected topic. These should be articles that have been published in professional journals, NOT POPULAR MAGAZINES.

For each of the three articles, print out a copy of the citation page from the database that you used. Then find a copy of the article. Turn in the **citation page** and **first page** of each of the articles.

Part II: Locating Internet Resources

Using what you learned in class about locating and evaluating Internet resources, locate three Web sites pertaining to your selected topic. Fill out one copy of the Web Site Evaluation Form that was provided in class for each Web site. Include the first page from each of the sites that you evaluated.

Complete the following checklist before submitting your assignment so that you know you have all the correct components:

—— Cover Sheet (your name, course name and number, assignment title, date).
—— Citation page for each research article (must submit 3).
—— First page of each research article (must submit 3).
—— First page of each Web site (must submit 3).
—— Web evaluation sheet for each of the Web sites (must submit 3).

Figure 11.3. Assignment for a Family Studies Course.

Source: Adapted with permission from Rhonda A. Richardson, School of Family and Consumer Studies, Kent State University.

It is generally best to get this type of feedback from students rather than your colleagues. Your peers may be oblivious to jargon (if there is any) or might have higher expectations for what students should know and should understand. Student assistants employed in the library can be good sources for feedback. If you do not have access to students, you can ask a colleague to look over your assignment, but stress the importance of approaching it from a student's perspective.

SCORING GUIDES

As you develop assignments it is important to keep in mind how you will assess them once they are completed. Taking the time to focus on the scoring of an assignment while you are developing it will make the assessment stronger and more meaningful for your students. Scoring guides are objective tools that can be used effectively for performance assessment. Creating scoring guides might seem challenging at first, but spending the time up front will actually save you time later when you are assessing multiple assignments. The process also forces you to examine how assignment components tie into learning objectives and to articulate which components you value the most. Again, while time consuming, this examination will actually help you focus your instruction on these components, ultimately resulting in improved student learning. Here are a few tips for creating three different scoring guides: checklists, rating scales, and rubrics.

Checklists

A checklist is simply a list of elements or behaviors that help establish minimum requirements for a project or assignment. The advantage of using a checklist is that it is easy to develop and use; the disadvantage is that a checklist does little to measure the quality of what is created.

A checklist can be used at a very basic level to help students assess whether they have all the components of an assignment. The sample assignment in Figure 11.3 includes such a checklist.

You could adapt the checklist that is given to your students by applying a scoring value to each component and then use it to help you assess whether a student has fulfilled the most basic requirements of the assignment (essentially, has she or he submitted all the required paper products). See Figure 11.4 for an example.

Number of points possible on assignment: 25

—— One cover sheet for the assignment including:
    —— student name (.25)
    —— course name and number (.25)
    —— assignment title (.25)
    —— date (.25)

—— Citation page for each research article (must submit 3)—2 pts. each.
—— First page of each research article (must submit 3)—2 pts. each.
—— First page of each Web site (must submit 3)—2 pts. each.
—— Web evaluation sheet for each of the Web sites (must submit 3)—2 pts. each.

Instructors could assign a numerical value to the components (for example, 2 points for each main item submitted and .25 points for each of the four main elements of the cover sheet). A student handing in only two Web evaluation sheets would get 4 points rather than the 6 required to fulfill the assignment in its entirety. A student who handed in 3 articles that were thought to be research articles, but were actually not, would get a score of zero for that category instead of 6 points. In this example, a "perfect" score would be 25.

Figure 11.4. Checklist for Assignment for a Family Studies Course.

The score on the checklist would only be used as one component of the grade. You would have to further evaluate the product itself to determine the final grade or score. The next two scoring guides offer an option for doing that.

Rating Scales

A checklist can have more value as an assessment tool if a rating scale is added. Rating scales consist of a continuum represented through numbers (for example, no. 1 through no. 5 with 5 being the best) or words (for example, *has included all, has included some, has not included any*). The rating scale in Figure 11.5 is one that has been developed to facilitate the process of Web site evaluation. Students in the hypothetical family studies course would be required to complete this form for each Web site evaluated and return it to the faculty member along with the first page of the Web site.

The rating scale helps students determine the degree of authority or accuracy of the information on the Web site. It does not, however, include specific criteria for judging whether a component should receive a 4 or a 1. While rating whether a Web site "displays correct grammar and punctuation," might be easy for students, it might be harder for them to assess whether an author "has a high level of expertise and experience related to the site's subject." Students would have to be provided with indicators that would help them judge an author's expertise or tools for verifying an author's background. With this information in hand, students could then more effectively use a rating scale to judge the author's authority. This is an example of how learning objectives for a course need to be tied to a scoring guide in order to be effective.

Once you have received the completed rating scales from the students, you will then need to assess the degree to which the students accurately evaluated the Web sites. One option for doing this would be to examine each of the Web sites reviewed by students and complete your own rating scale for the sites. You could then compare the students' rating scales to your own and score their assignments accordingly. You can imagine, however, how time consuming this would be if you used this assignment with a class of 30 students—you would be examining 90 Web sites! To address this workload issue, you could have students select three Web sites from a list of 15 or 20 that you have already evaluated. If you are worried about students illicitly borrowing from each other's work, have them do the exercise in class, perhaps even with a partner.

If you decide, however, to stick with the original plan of having each student select his or her own Web sites, you might need to rely more on the checklist approach to evaluate whether a student successfully completed the assignment. Essentially, students receive credit just for submitting all the proper components of the assignment.

An alternative would be to do some kind of holistic assessment of the students' performance on the assignment. In this case, you might rely on your own experience with Web sites and domain names to assess whether the student took the assignment seriously and selectively check students' work. For example, a "red flag" might go up if you notice a student giving a high overall score to a personal Web site touting the therapeutic value of tobacco smoke. Because this goes against most common medical evidence, you might choose to check out the Web site and compare your impression to that of the student.

Web Site Name:

Web Site URL:

Circle the appropriate score for each of the criteria on the left.

	Strongly Agree	Agree	Disagree	Strongly Disagree
Authority				
Author has a high level of expertise and experience related to the site's subject.	4	3	2	1
Web site has a strong affiliation with a credible organization.	4	3	2	1
Purpose and objectivity				
The purpose and intent of the site is clear, including any bias or particular viewpoint.	4	3	2	1
On this site, facts are presented as facts and opinions are presented as opinions.	4	3	2	1
Accuracy				
This site displays correct grammar and punctuation. Words are spelled correctly.	4	3	2	1
The information on this site is accurate and well documented.	4	3	2	1
Additional research supports the information on this site.	4	3	2	1
Web sites linked from this site appear credible.	4	3	2	1
Currency				
The information on this site is current.	4	3	2	1
The Web site has been updated recently.	4	3	2	1
Usability				
The site is well organized and easy to navigate.	4	3	2	1
The links, images, and other media on this site are present and working.	4	3	2	1
Total the scores circled in each column:				

The final score for this Web site is: _____

Figure 11.5. Rating Scale for Web Site Evaluation.

	Superior A	Very Good B	Acceptable C	Borderline D	Unacceptable F
Author fulfills the assignment with respect to length.					
Changes suggested by professor properly implemented.					
Author presents a clear central idea and coherent topic statement.					
Support material is incorporated logically and insightfully.					
Paraphrasing is properly used to support the thesis.					
Organization and structure are evident and logical.					
There are clear transitions between each paragraph or section.					
There is a variety of sentence structure and interesting word choice.					
Introduction and conclusion effectively relate to the goal of the paper.					
Reference list uses proper APA citation style.					
There are few, if any, sentence structure, grammatical, mechanical, or spelling errors.					

Grading Criteria:
   A: No discernable problems in this area so that readability and quality are outstanding
   B: Only a few discernable problems in this area so that readability and quality remain acceptable
   C: Some discernable problems that clearly affect readability and quality
   D: A sufficient number of discernable problems so that readability and quality are significantly impaired
   F: So many problems that readability and quality are severely undermined

Figure 11.6. Rating Scale for a Paper for a Psychology Course.

Source: Adapted with permission from Amy Jo Stavnezer, Department of Psychology, College of Wooster.

Another example of a rating scale is provided in Figure 11.6. This type of scale can be used to assess how well a student did on specific components of a short paper. The rating scale ranges from "superior" to "unacceptable" which corresponds to the letter grades "A" to "F." To use this kind of rating scale, you read the paper and then judge it according to the criteria for the paper (for example, "there are clear transitions between each paragraph or section"). If there were "no discernible problems in this area," a checkmark would go in the "superior" column. If there were so many problems with transitions that the "readability and quality were significantly impaired," a checkmark would go in the "borderline" category. A preponderance of checkmarks in the "superior" column would earn the student an "A." Too many checkmarks in the "borderline" column would result in a "D" grade.

You can see that there is a wide range in the use and effectiveness of checklists and rating scales. If you want to provide students with more specific details of what is expected in a product, consider developing a rubric.

Rubrics

Rubrics provide a way of measuring the degree to which a particular skill has been mastered, used, or incorporated into a bigger process. A rubric provides detailed descriptions of how separate parts of products or performances will be assessed and assigns a score to each part. These individual component scores are then added for a total score. The added detail and description of performance levels helps rubrics overcome the shortcomings of checklists and rating scales. A rubric establishes criteria for how work will be judged and allows students to gain a better understanding of areas in which they need to improve or in which they excel. By establishing benchmarks (clear guidelines as to what is excellent or superior work), a rubric also demonstrates to students what they need to do in order to improve. Rubrics should be used in a context of continuous improvement. They provide a quick and easy way for students to self-assess and provide the instructor with a method of gauging process. They also allow instructors to be consistent in the grading process.

A rubric is made up of three essential components: criteria, indicators of quality, and scoring technique.

1. Evaluative Criteria or Objectives. These are the criteria by which the product will be assessed. They might include categories such as organization, proper use of citation style, or variety of sources. Ask yourself, what general indicators will be used to judge the product?
2. Level and Definition of Quality. These two components go hand-in-hand. Under each of the evaluative criteria, you will need to decide on what levels of quality you want to use. Generally rubrics will have from three to five levels. For example, if one of the criteria is "uses a variety of sources," you might create five levels: superior, above average, average, below average, unacceptable. See Figure 11.7 for examples of other levels.

    When creating a rubric it is useful to first identify the qualities you seek at each level. When possible, solicit input from your colleagues as to what constitutes superior or excellent work, what constitutes just average work, and what constitutes below average or poor work. If you choose to have three levels in your rubric this will provide you with the foundation from which to build. If you choose to have five levels in your rubric, you will then

In a rubric, there are typically three to five levels of achievement. There are many different labels that are used for rubrics in addition to a simple number ranking system of 1–3 or 1–5 or traditional letter grades such as A to F.

Some examples of labels used in rubrics include:

Unacceptable, Satisfactory, Exemplary
Poor, Average, Excellent
Advanced, Proficient, Partially proficient, Beginning
Excellent, Very good, Adequate, Needs attention
Complete evidence, Partial evidence, Minimal evidence, No evidence
Accomplished, Proficient, Novice
Expert publisher, Apprentice publisher, Novice publisher, Needs mentoring
Exceeds standard, Meets standard, Approaching standard, Below standard
Superior, Above average, Average, Below average, Unacceptable
Distinguished, Proficient, Emerging, Unacceptable

Figure 11.7. Labeling the Levels of a Rubric.

need to look at what constitutes work that is between poor and average and between average and excellent.

A very simple example of this application would be deciding that a paper that uses a mix of scholarly and popular articles, books, reference sources, and Web sites would be judged as "superior," while a paper that uses only Web sites and one book might be evaluated as "below average." To further help students understand what is meant by these labels, the description should include specific indicators. The description for "superior" might have these descriptions: "no more than one-third of references come from one type of resource" or "maximum of 2 chapters from the same book."

There are many different ways in which you can set up your rubric grid. Heidi Goodrich Andrade (2000, p. 16) suggests using the following as guidelines for establishing criteria at four different levels:

Yes—Absolutely and completely meets the criteria with no exceptions.
Yes, but—Meets the majority of the criteria, but there are some
            exceptions/areas in which there is need for improvement.
No, but—Primarily fails to meet the criteria, except in a few areas.
No—Absolutely does not meet the criteria.

You could then substitute labels. For example, "Yes" could be "excellent," "Yes, but" could become "good," "No, but" could become "poor," and "No" could become "unacceptable."

It is important that the levels of a rubric provide substantive detail so that students can clearly identify what is needed to move up the performance ladder. The descriptions need to be specific. On the other hand, the rubric should not be so lengthy or detailed that it it is seen

	5	4	3	2	1	Score
Topic Statement	Your topic is very clear and focused. Scope and related terms are thoroughly discussed.	Your topic is clear and focused. Scope and related terms are adequately discussed.	Your topic is somewhat clear and somewhat focused. Discussion of scope lacks clarity and/or thoroughness. Some related terms have been overlooked.	Your topic is somewhat clear and lacks focus. Scope is not discussed. Few, if any, related terms are identified.	Your topic is absent or very unclear and lacks any focus.	
Authority	You identify the author(s) of your sources and they are credible.	You identify the author(s) of your sources and most of them are credible.	You identify the author(s) of most of your sources and some of them are credible.	You identify the author(s) of some of your sources and a few of them are credible.	You identify the author(s) of few, if any, of your sources; and their credibility is in doubt or unclear.	
Currency/ Relevancy	Your sources are current and highly relevant to your topic.	Your sources are current and mostly relevant to your topic.	Most of your sources are current, but a few are of questionable relevance to your topic.	Some of your sources are current, and less than half are relevant to your topic.	Your sources are not current and only a few, if any, are relevant to your topic.	
Documen- tation	You correctly document your sources using MLA Documenta- tion Style.	You correctly document most of your sources using MLA Documentat- ion Style.	You correctly document about half of your sources using MLA Documentat- ion Style.	You correctly document a few of your sources using MLA Documentat- ion Style or you follow another documentation style.	You do not correctly document many of your sources, or it is not clear which documentation style you followed.	

Annotations	You write brief, yet clear annotations for all of your sources.	You write brief, yet clear annotations for most of your sources.	You write annotations for most of your sources, but they are wordy and not always clear.	You write annotations for only about half of your sources. They are sometimes too brief or too long and not always clear.	You write only a few annotations, if any, and it is not clear if you actually reviewed your source materials.	
Mechanics	Your bibliography is free of major errors in grammar, punctuation, and spelling.	Your bibliography has a few errors in grammar, punctuation, or spelling.	Your bibliography has several errors in grammar, punctuation, or spelling that indicate carelessness.	Your bibliography has several, often repeated errors in grammar, punctuation, or spelling that may distract the reader.	Your bibliography is difficult to read because of the high number of errors in grammar, punctuation, or spelling.	
TOTAL SCORE (30 POSSIBLE POINTS)						

Figure 11.8. Example of a Rubric for Assessing an Annotated Bibliography Assignment.

as overwhelming and therefore not used. See Figure 11.8 for an example of an effective rubric for an annotated bibliography.

3. Scoring Strategy. While the descriptions provide you and the students with specific criteria that need to be addressed in the assignment, you will typically want to assign a number value to each of the component parts in order to come up with a final score. The point value will vary depending on how well the criteria for that component are met. In a five-level rubric, the highest level might be assigned the number 5 or 4 and the lowest level assigned the number 1 or 0, depending on the labels used. If the lowest level is described as a complete absence, then a score of zero seems appropriate.

Online Rubric Tools

If you are feeling hesitant about creating a rubric, you might want to try out one of the many Web-based tools available. Figure 11.9 provides links to several sites that will provide you with a foundation from which to build. Although many of these tools have been created for the K-12 environment, they can be easily adapted to projects that are regularly assigned in college courses.

Rubistar—http://rubistar.4teachers.org/index.php.

Rubric Builder—http://landmark-project.com/classweb/tools/rubric_builder.php.

teAchnology Rubric Creator—www.teach-nology.com/web_tools/rubrics/.
Requires annual membership fee.

Figure 11.9. Online Rubric Tools.

——— The assignment prompt includes some introductory text.
——— All instructions in the prompt are clear and focused on the objectives of the assignment.
——— All learning objectives are included in the scoring rubric.
——— Examples of a high quality product or a highly scored rubric are provided.

Figure 11.10. Performance Assessment Checklist.

Setting Clear Expectations

For a rubric to be an effective tool in the learning process, students must be given access to the rubric before they begin work on the assignment. Go over the rubric with them so that they have a clear understanding of what kind of work constitutes a high score on each section of the rubric. Consider distributing an example of an exceptional assignment from an earlier class to serve as a model for your current students to follow. (You will need to obtain permission from the student whose work you will be sharing.) If this is the first time you have given the assignment, then you can create an example yourself. Just make sure that it is done from the perspective of a proficient student, and not that of an information literacy instructor!

Keep in mind that even the most detailed and thorough assignments and scoring guides will only be effective if you have aligned your instruction with the learning objectives that you are assessing. Figure 11.10 provides a brief checklist of the key components of a performance assignment.

ANALYZING DATA FROM PERFORMANCE ASSESSMENTS

Scoring guides bring objectivity to complex assignments by providing the instructor with clear guidelines for scoring. Once the product has been scored, both the total score and the scoring guide should be shared with the student. Simply providing a score on the assignment offers very little in the way of useful feedback. Students who are shown where they fall on the continuum of scoring criteria are better able to use that information for future improvement.

Scoring guides can also provide you, the instructor, with a snapshot of class performance, and allow you to identify overall strengths and weaknesses of students. If students consistently performed poorly on a specific aspect of an assignment (the topic statement or documentation, for example) you may want to investigate the instruction you provided on this skill. It may be an indication that your learning objective for this aspect of the performance was not met. This is an opportunity to reflect on your instructional approach and perhaps try a new method.

ARE PERFORMANCE ASSESSMENTS RIGHT FOR YOU?

Review the following factors when considering performance assessments:

 Time

Performance assessments require a significant time commitment, both in terms of the assignment design and in terms of the classroom time that needs to be set aside to do the assessment. Time must also be built in for the development of the scoring guide, especially as it relates to the learning objectives.

 Money

There are few costs (other than time) associated with performance assessment. Assessing processes may require some resources if you are taking advantage of usability labs or need to employ graduate assistants to help observe performance. Recording performance assessments (either through audio or video) might require a financial investment if equipment needs to be rented or bought.

 Level of Assessment

Performance assessment is generally done at the classroom level. It is used to measure how students in a particular course have mastered material. It could also be used in programmatic assessment if products or processes were compared across courses.

 Assessment Domain

Performance assessments work in the behavioral domain. They allow us to evaluate how well students can apply knowledge and perform skills, but will not tell us systematically what students know or what they think or feel. Performance assessments work best on specific problems, focused on specific skills. Consider a combination of performance and knowledge assessments to gain a fuller assessment picture of students.

 Access to Participants

Whether assessing a product or process, you will need to work closely with classroom faculty for access to their students and their students' products.

 Level of Faculty Collaboration

Because performance assessments generally center on assignments, they often require a high level of faculty-librarian collaboration both for access to students and for access to the assignments. You will need advice, input, and permission from faculty instructors to design effective scoring guides and rubrics, which in turn means you will have to collaborate on establishing agreed-upon learning outcomes. For this reason performance assessments often work very well in situations where strong collaborative relationships already exist.

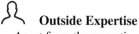 **Outside Expertise**

Apart from the expertise of collaborating faculty members, performance assessments usually do not require outside consultation with experts. Of course, workshops, seminars, and further reading can help, but in most cases, you will need to develop your own expertise related to the assessment of a specific assignment.

WORKS CITED AND FURTHER READING

Andrade, H. G. (2000). Using rubrics to promote thinking and learning. *Educational Leadership, 57*(5), 13–18.

Association of College and Research Libraries (ACRL). (2000). *Information literacy competency standards for higher education: Standards, performance indicators, and outcomes*. Retrieved May 23, 2006 from www.ala.org/ala/acrl/acrlstandards/informationliteracycompetency.htm.

Blattner, N. H. and Frazier, C. L. (2002). Developing a performance-based assessment of students' critical thinking skills. *Assessing Writing, 8*(1), 47–64.

Brualdi, A. (1998). Implementing performance assessment in the classroom. *Practical Assessment, Research, and Evaluation, 6*(2). Retrieved March 20, 2007 from http://PAREonline.net/getvn.asp?v=6&n=2.

Holloway, R. E., Doyle, C. S., and Lindsay, J. (1997). *Performance based assessment for information literacy*. A paper presented at Treasure Mountain VI Conference, March 31–April 1, 1997. ERIC Document Reproduction Service No. ED 408938.

Huba, M. E. and Freed, J. E. (2000). Using rubrics to provide feedback to students. *Learner-centered assessment on college campuses: Shifting the focus from teaching to learning*. Boston, MA: Allyn and Bacon (pp. 151–200).

Mertler, C. A. (2003). *Classroom assessment: A practical guide for educators*. Los Angeles, CA: Pyrczak Publishing.

Oosterhof, A. (2001). *Classroom applications of educational measurement*. Upper Saddle River, NJ: Merrill.

Suskie, L. (2004). *Assessing student learning: A common sense guide*. Bolton, MA: Anker Publishing.

12

Portfolios

Indicators:

 Requires a significant time commitment

 Requires little money, unless using electronic portfolios

 Level of assessment: Classroom, Programmatic, Institutional

 Domains: Affective, Behavioral, Cognitive

 Access to participants: Requires considerable effort to maintain contact with participants

 Requires intense collaboration with faculty

 No outside expertise needed, unless using electronic portfolios

Key Characteristics:

- Provides an in-depth assessment of how information literacy competencies are applied.
- Assesses skills over time.
- Allows for individual differences in expression.
- Requires long-term access to students.
- Requires collaboration between student and instructor.
- Requires high effort on the part of the student (creation) and instructor (evaluation).
- May involve complex infrastructure if electronic portfolios are used.

AN OVERVIEW OF PORTFOLIOS

In an educational context, a portfolio is a collection of works assembled around a common theme. Portfolios include both products (such as essays, research logs, and lesson plans) and reflective pieces. Traditionally associated with the K-12 curriculum, they are increasingly being used in higher education as part of programmatic and institutional assessment efforts. For librarians, portfolios offer a rare opportunity for a comprehensive look at students' information literacy competencies as well as their development of these skills over time.

Although portfolios generally have some common characteristics, there is no one single model that must be followed. Portfolios can be designed to collect assignments for an individual class or to reflect learning that has taken place throughout a student's college career. They can be used as evidence that students have mastered the institution's general education requirements or that they have met criteria for professional licensing. They can be made up of a collection of hard copy assignments or they can use an electronic interface for storage and feedback.

Portfolios provide instructors with feedback as to which areas students struggle with. They provide information on how information literacy skills have been applied or ignored. They force students to step through a process that, given a choice, many would rather avoid. They can also help reduce plagiarism because students are often required to document a process through reflection.

As a librarian, you are most likely to use portfolios in one of the following contexts:

- You are teaching an information literacy or library skills course.
- You are co-teaching a "non-library" course with a faculty member or have a good working relationship with a faculty member who is using portfolio assessment.
- You are a liaison to a department that uses portfolios as part of programmatic assessment.
- Your institution has made information literacy assessment a component of student portfolios.

WHAT GOES INTO A PORTFOLIO?

Regardless of context, portfolios generally include the following three elements:

1. A checklist of items to be included: This checklist will vary depending on the purpose of the portfolio, but it should always be as specific as possible, providing students with guidelines on format, deadlines for submission, and so on.

2. The products themselves: A portfolio can include a wide range of products: bibliographies, short stories, essays, brochures, artwork, videos, research papers, lesson plans, etc. Depending on the context, the number of products is typically from four to eight. It is generally recommended that writing products be a maximum of two or three pages in length (unless the portfolio is to include a research paper or final project). One reason for this restriction is to keep the evaluation manageable. Remember that you might be evaluating multiple portfolios and you want to be able to provide quality feedback on each one. Students will also be able to more easily manage a smaller set of products.

3. At least one reflective piece: Reflection is integral to a portfolio. Without it, a portfolio is nothing more than a folder stuffed with assignments. Students can be asked to reflect on the creation of one of their products or to do more holistic reflection of the entire creative process. According to John Zubizarreta (2004, p. 28) a learning portfolio provides the student with "an opportunity to engage in self-examination of what has been learned in an assignment, a course, or a program; how it has been applied; why the learning has been valuable; and to what extent the product of learning meets educational standards and goals."

As a rule, students do not have a lot of experience with the art of reflection. It is something that needs to be modeled and developed as a skill over time. To facilitate the process, it is important to provide students with specific questions meant to trigger reflection rather than an open-ended command to "reflect on this assignment." Portfolio Item No. 8 in Figure 12.1 below provides examples of questions that can assist students in the reflection process.

CREATING THE PORTFOLIO ASSIGNMENT

If you choose to assess students' work through the use of a portfolio, you will need to decide on the context and the exact components. Think about what it is that you want students to learn (the objectives for the project or course) and determine how the artifacts to be included in the portfolio will show evidence of that learning. Remember that you will also want to integrate a reflective component into the portfolio.

The example in Figure 12.1 is based on an English course in which students write a research paper. This type of assignment involves the use of many information literacy skills and provides multiple opportunities for reflection. This particular project also lends itself to collaboration with faculty in terms of doing instruction and in participating in the evaluation of the products.

The portfolio components described in Figure 12.1 provide you and the faculty member with an assessment of the student's information literacy skills. They can help identify areas in which students struggle and those in which they excel. They allow you the opportunity to follow up with additional information and instruction during the research process or to adjust your instruction in future classes. The portfolio components also document the critical thinking process that is taking place as students prepare to write the research paper. The holistic reflection that is required at the end of the process forces students to reflect on their own learning and to think about how skills can be transferred to other applications.

Remember that while the assignments in the portfolio provide you with valuable information, it is very likely that students will be resistant to what they see as extra work being imposed on them, especially if they have heavy workloads in other classes. It is critically important to help students understand the context for portfolios and how they can contribute to student learning. You must convince students that this is not busy work, and that by documenting the process they will be able to receive feedback and assistance before the final paper is due. Figure 12.2 shows you the complete checklist for the portfolio. Students would also receive specific assignment prompts for each component. See Chapter 11 for more information on effective assignment design.

PROGRAMMATIC AND INSTITUTIONAL ASSESSMENT

The example above illustrates how products can be collected in a portfolio to show the progression of student work throughout a semester course. Portfolios can also be used

---

The Scenario

You are working with a faculty member in the English Department who has assigned her students an informational research paper focusing on a current social problem of interest to the student. In a 10–12 page paper, students must provide background information on the topic and explore multiple aspects of the problem. The main goals of the course are to improve students' abilities to synthesize information and to effectively incorporate that information into a research paper.

The Faculty Member Wants Students to:

- know how to write an effective thesis statement;
- be able to support that thesis statement with reliable evidence in a well-constructed paper;
- use reliable sources;
- be able to properly cite those sources.

As a Librarian You Want Students to:

- be aware that they routinely use their own knowledge as a foundation for writing;
- know how to find the information they need;
- be able to evaluate the information they locate;
- know how one resource can lead to finding other sources of information.

In the past, when the faculty member has taught this course, the main assignments have been an annotated bibliography, a Web site evaluation form, a rough draft of the paper, and the final paper. You and the faculty member discuss the importance of assessing the process that students go through to create these products and choose to have the students create a portfolio of their work.

Step 1: Breaking Down the Assignments

Your first task is to decide what is going to be included in the portfolio. Items include the four assignments above (the annotated bibliography, the Web site evaluation form, the rough draft, and the final paper). These, however, are end products and do not demonstrate the process or how students felt about the work. To turn the portfolio into a better assessment tool, you will need to break down the assignments into component parts and look for logical places where students could demonstrate their information literacy skills.

Let's use the annotated bibliography as an example. The instructions to the students for this assignment are as follows:

- Select five sources to annotate, including at least one scholarly article, at least one article from a popular magazine or newspaper, and at least one chapter from an edited book or article from a reference book. Web sites from the public Web may be used in the paper, but should not be included in this assignment.
- The citations must be in MLA citation style.
- Each annotation must be two to three paragraphs. The annotation should summarize the main points of the article. The abstract that came with the article may NOT be used as the summary.
- Mention at least one lead that you can use from the article for further research (names of researchers, associations, references, etc.).

Now think about the process that students must go through to fulfill this assignment.

1. Before they begin the annotated bibliography (or any part of the paper), they must first decide on a general topic.
2. They must then focus the topic so that it is manageable for a 10–12 page paper.
3. They must then locate the sources to be included in the annotated bibliography.
4. Next they need to evaluate those sources to determine whether they fit the requirements of the assignment and whether the information provided is appropriate for the paper.
5. They need to read the articles and chapters and jot down key points for the summary.
6. They need to look through the articles for clues that could lead them to other sources (quotes from researchers, the names of organizations doing work on the topic, references at the end of the article, etc.).
7. They need to put the citations into MLA format and verify that they have done so correctly.
8. They need to pull all of these elements together into the required format for the annotated bibliography.

Although there are many parts to this assignment, typically only the final product is submitted and graded. By having students show evidence that they have followed the above steps, you will be able to more effectively document the process and be able to evaluate specific information literacy skills.

Step 2: Identifying Portfolio Components

To identify portfolio components, translate the above steps into tangible products. For example, steps 1 and 2 above relate to topic selection and could be documented by having students write a reflective piece.

Portfolio Item #1: Reflection on Topic Selection

In one page, reflect on how you selected your topic. What made you choose the topic that you did? Just saying that the topic was interesting is not enough. Instead, explain what interested you about the topic and what personal experiences may have influenced your decision. Did you consider several different topics before settling on this one? If so, why did you rule the others out? How does this topic meet the criteria for the research paper? In addition to answering these questions, include at least two sentences summarizing what you already know about the topic (either through your own experience or through what you have heard or read through the media).

Portfolio Item #2: Search Strategy

During the library instruction session, you were shown how to break down your thesis statement into key concepts as a way of preparing for searching for articles and books. Include one search history from a database or catalog search that demonstrates the keywords that you used in your search and how you combined them together. Make sure to identify where you did the search (name of database, online catalog, etc.).

Portfolio Item #3: Annotated Bibliography

The assignment requirements for this item were outlined earlier in Step 1.

Portfolio Item #4: Reflection on Source Selection for Annotated Bibliography

This is your opportunity to justify your selection of the five sources in your annotated bibliography and also to provide information on any difficulties you had in finding material. For each item, explain why you thought the resource should be included. What was it about the resource that made you think it would be useful? Did it provide extensive background information on your topic? Did it help support one of the points you want to make in your paper? Was it easy to read?

Be honest about difficulties you had. If you felt pressure to complete the assignment and are not happy with the sources you chose, then include this information in your paper. Do not, however, just write, "I couldn't find anything." Explain why you think you couldn't find a good article (for example, you need more help in searching the databases, or you don't understand how to find reference books).

Finally, your reflection must include one paragraph explaining what information you think you still need to write your research paper.

Portfolio Item #5: Rough Draft of the Paper

The rough draft should demonstrate that you have made significant progress in your research and writing process. As the final paper is expected to be from 10–12 pages, your rough draft should be at least five to six pages. If you are still doing research on one aspect of your paper, indicate this in an explanatory note attached to your rough draft. In other words, explain what it is that you still need to add to your paper and make a note of any information you are still trying to obtain. Your rough draft will be given to one of your classmates for peer review prior to inclusion in the portfolio.

Portfolio Item #6: Peer Review of Rough Draft

Include the comments that were made by one of your classmates as part of the peer review process of your rough draft.

Portfolio Item #7: Final Paper

Follow guidelines for paper formatting. Paper must be in MLA format.

Portfolio Item #8: Reflection on Research Paper

This writing assignment is a final reflective piece on the process and should be one to two pages in length. You are expected to comment on your own experiences with the overall research and writing process. Be honest. Use these questions as guidelines for your reflection:

- What did you like or not like about the timetable for the project?
- What did you like or not like about the assignments you were expected to submit? Why?
- What difficulties (if any) did you encounter in your research?
- What could have helped you do better research?
- What did you learn from doing the research paper and associated assignments?
- What advice would you offer to students who are assigned a similar project?
- How could this project be improved?
- What skills did you learn that you think will help you in other courses?

Figure 12.1. Example of a Portfolio Assignment.

Each submitted item must be accompanied by a cover sheet that includes the following information: Student Name, Date, and Name of the Assignment.

—— **#1 Reflection on Topic Selection** (due February 12)

> 1 page double-spaced; in addition to several paragraphs explaining topic selection, reflection must include at least two sentences summarizing what you already know about the topic.

—— **#2 Search Strategy** (due February 19)

> Search history printout from online catalog or research database.

—— **#3 Annotated Bibliography** (due February 28)

> - Five sources—at least one scholarly article; at least one popular magazine or newspaper article; at least one chapter from edited book or reference book.
> - Citations in MLA style.
> - Each annotation must be two to three paragraphs.
> - Each annotation must summarize main points; include one lead from each source.

—— **#4 Reflection on Source Selection for the Annotated Bibliography**
(due February 28)

> One paragraph on each of the five sources. Sixth paragraph explains what information you still need to complete the research for your paper.

—— **#5 Rough Draft of Paper** (due March 31)

> Five to six pages minimum; may include explanatory note indicating what sources you still need to complete the paper.

—— **#6 Peer Review of Rough draft** (due March 31)

> Comment sheet from peer review of rough draft; attach to rough draft.

—— **#7 Final Paper** (due April 26)

> Must use MLA formatting; follow guideline sheet distributed in class.

—— **#8 Reflection on Research Paper Process** (due April 28)

> One to two pages in length; use guidelines for reflection distributed in class.

Figure 12.2. Example of a Checklist of a Research Paper Portfolio.

in both programmatic and institutional assessment as evidence that specific outcomes or skills have been met. In this context, students can be asked to collect examples of their work throughout their academic career. Contrasting student work from a first-year English class with work completed as part of a writing-intensive capstone course in their majors can provide a significant opportunity to assess the development of information literacy skills (particularly if students are expected to complete similar assignments in both classes).

Students in teacher education programs have been doing portfolios for years, often aligning them with professional standards. Categories for which students are required to submit evidence might include instructional planning, communication, diversity, or instructional strategies. Students in graduate programs might submit portfolio components that demonstrate that they have acquired a specified set of proficiencies or skills.

If you are a librarian who has a good working relationship with education faculty, you might want to suggest that an information literacy assessment component be introduced into the portfolio checklist. For example, a student could be asked to develop a lesson plan for teaching seventh graders how to do Web evaluation. Or education students could be required to develop an annotated bibliography of sources that could be used by a new teacher who is working with students who have reading difficulties.

Colleges and universities have also been using portfolios as a tool to help students reflect on their overall learning throughout their academic career. Institutions that require students to meet general education outcomes may have students include evidence in a portfolio that they have met those requirements.

When a portfolio is used for programmatic or institutional assessment, students are often given a choice of what they want to include, within parameters. For example, from 2003 through 2006 Mansfield University in Pennsylvania required undergraduate students to submit a General Education Portfolio. The portfolio included five pieces of work chosen by the student and a sixth product that was chosen by the instructor of one of the English courses. The submitted "artifacts" were required to address at least one of the General Education Outcomes (critical thinking, problem solving, analysis, communication) and needed to be spread across at least four of the five General Education Blocks (humanities, natural sciences, languages and literature, social sciences, and mathematics). As you can imagine, keeping track of all of these items for each student took a great deal of effort and organization. Mansfield used a General Education Artifact Cover Sheet for each artifact in the portfolios (see Figure 12.3).

Cover Sheet

Directions: Complete the information on this form and attach a cover sheet to each artifact in your portfolio.

Student Name: _____

Student ID Number: _____

This artifact meets the following General Education Outcomes: (Check at least one.)
_____ Critical Thinking   _____ Analysis
_____ Problem Solving   _____ Communication

Check the General Education Block where you did this artifact: (Indicate which General Education Block this artifact represents.)
_____ Humanities   _____ Languages and Literature   _____ Mathematics
_____ Natural Sciences   _____ Social Sciences   _____ Core

Course and Number: (e.g., MA 2231–02) _____

Semester: (e.g., SP 2006) _____

Instructor's signature: (Signature must be obtained during the semester the course is taught.)

_____   _____
              (Print name)   (Signature)

Figure 12.3. General Education Artifact Cover Sheet.

Source: General Education Portfolio Template, Mansfield University, 2003–2006.

COLLECTING THE MATERIAL

When you think of portfolios, you might have a mental image of an advertising major going for her first job interview accompanied by a thick black binder filled with examples of her work. Or an artist pulling out digital images of his work from a large folder as he tries to convince a gallery owner to exhibit his artwork. Research assignments don't have the same panache as artwork, but students should be encouraged to collect the portfolio assignments as they are returned and to turn them in collectively at the end of the semester. Those students who need a creative outlet can be encouraged to submit the materials in decorated binders or, as they have been used by some teachers, unused pizza boxes! One faculty member actually requests that students submit their work in a folder rather than a binder, so that he can more easily pull out the components (without having to unsnap and snap binder rings). In terms of assessment, the contents matter more than the container they come in, but it doesn't hurt to encourage students to think about their work as part of a greater whole and to take pride in the project.

ELECTRONIC PORTFOLIOS

Although assembling a folder of work done over one semester seems very doable, students may find it organizationally challenging to have to collect papers and artifacts throughout their college careers. Likewise, those who are at the receiving end of the collection may also find the prospect overwhelming. A faculty member in a college of education at one university commented on the daunting task of hauling home over-flowing three-ring binders that filled the trunk of her car, each of which needed to be graded and critiqued. Stories such as these are just one of the reasons that institutions are moving toward the adoption of electronic portfolios or e-portfolios.

The purchase, set up, and management of an electronic portfolio system takes considerable time and resources. This is rarely something that would be done by a librarian or library without institutional support. If you are aware of departments on your campus that are using electronic portfolios, consider exploring ways in which information literacy assessment could be incorporated.

If you are interested in learning more about e-portfolios, you might want to begin by checking out the report written by George Lorenzo and John Ittelson (2005) on behalf of the EDUCAUSE Learning Initiative (available at www.educause.edu/ir/library/pdf/ELI3001.pdf). It provides a very useful overview of how electronic portfolios are being used in higher education, as well as links to examples at various institutions. Other examples can be found on a site created to support the SUNY Conference on E-Portfolios (2006) (www.brockport.edu/eportfolio).

ASSESSING PORTFOLIOS

In addition to providing students with details on the portfolio assignments and a checklist of due dates and contents, it is important that students understand how their work will be assessed. A portfolio assignment should ideally be accompanied by a scoring rubric that explains in detail the components of the assignment and your expectations for completion. (Rubrics are covered in Chapter 12 of this book.) Keep in mind that you may have a rubric for each product in the portfolio as well as a rubric that is used to assess the portfolio in its entirety. In our sample portfolio, the instructor might want to use

Linda Suskie wisely advises that your goals for the portfolio determine how you will evaluate it. In other words, first decide on what you want your students to achieve and then create a rubric to evaluate the products. Here are four areas to consider:

If your goals include <u>assessing student progress in achieving major course or program learning goals</u>, use a rubric that lists those goals and criteria for acceptable performance.

If your goals include <u>encouraging metacognition</u> (learning how to learn by reflecting on the learning process), evaluate the portfolios in terms of the effort students put into self-reflection.

If your goals include <u>encouraging students to improve their performance</u>, have students include drafts in their portfolios, and evaluate the portfolios in terms of improvement.

If your goals include <u>encouraging risk-taking and creativity</u>, evaluate the portfolios in terms of the reflections students provide on the risks they took in their work.

Figure 12.4. Linking Goals to Evaluation.

Source: Linda Suskie, *Assessing Student Learning: A Common Sense Guide*, 2004.

a simple rating scale for some of the items (like the search strategy) and a more complete rubric for the others (like the final paper). See Figure 11.8 (Chapter 11) for an example of a rubric that could be used to assess an annotated bibliography.

How you create the rubrics for your portfolio will depend on the goals for the course and the value you place on different aspects of student learning. Figure 12.4 lists suggestions for the types of rubrics to consider.

ARE PORTFOLIOS RIGHT FOR YOU?

Students may feel overwhelmed by having to create a portfolio and your assistance and involvement will be more intense than with many of the other assessment tools described in this book. You may be a partner with faculty to grade assignments and/or provide one-on-one or group instruction. Keep this in mind in terms of your workload issues.

 Time

Portfolios require a greater investment of time than many of the other assessment tools mentioned in this book. If you are using portfolio assessment for the first time, you will find yourself spending a considerable amount of time managing the process, from the selection of portfolio components to the scoring of the product. Institutions requiring students to do portfolios also need to take into consideration the time that will be expended by faculty and staff to meet with students about the process and to monitor student participation.

 Money

Although there is very little cost involved with print portfolios, electronic portfolio software can be expensive. There may also be salary costs associated with the setup and management of the software. As a rule, however, those costs would not come out of library budgets.

 Level of Assessment

Portfolios can be used at all levels of assessment. Although portfolios would not be appropriate if you are primarily involved in one-shot instruction, they would work if you partner with faculty to provide information literacy instruction across a semester because they provide a vehicle for collecting multiple assignments. Portfolios are commonly used for classroom, programmatic, and institutional assessment.

 **Assessment Domains**

Portfolios offer assessment opportunities in all three domains. As a collection of products, portfolios provide you with information about how students perform (behavioral). As most portfolios include a reflective component, they also help you assess students' knowledge (cognitive) as well as their perceptions and feelings (affective).

 Access to Participants

Portfolios can be used for assessment only when you have ongoing access to students.

 Level of Faculty Collaboration

A high level of collaboration with faculty will be needed if you are to use a portfolio in your assessment program. If you are teaching a course on your own, this might not be necessary, unless evidence from the course is required for a programmatic or institutional portfolio. In those cases, you might need to work with faculty or administrators to make sure that your assignments meet portfolio criteria.

 Outside Expertise

Traditional portfolios do not require outside consultation with experts. Electronic portfolios may require support from systems or administrative personnel.

WORKS CITED AND FURTHER READING

Fast, M. and Armstrong, J. (2003). The course portfolio in a library setting. *Research Strategies, 19*, 46–56.

Lorenzo, G. and Ittelson, J. (2005). An overview of e-portfolios. *EDUCAUSE Learning Initiative*. www.educause.edu/ir/library/pdf/ELI3001.pdf.

Siemens, G. (2004). ePortfolios. *elearnspace*. www.elearnspace.org/Articles/eportfolios.htm.

Snavely, L. L. and Wright, C. A. (2003). Research portfolio use in undergraduate honors education: Assessment tool and model for future work. *The Journal of Academic Librarianship, 29*(5), 298–303.

SUNY Conference on E-portfolios. (2006). *Student samples.* www.brockport.edu/eportfolio/
    StudentSamples.html.
Suskie, L. (2004). *Assessing student learning: A common sense guide.* Bolton, MA:
    Anker Publishing.
Zubizarreta, J. (2004). *The learning portfolio: Reflective practice for improving student learning.*
    Bolton, MA: Anker Publishing.

Part III

What to Do with the Information

13

Analyzing the Data

This chapter is for those who want to go beyond the basic analytical processes described in each chapter in the "Tools" section. For several tools, there are options for more advanced analysis of the data. We will focus on two types of analysis: content analysis and descriptive statistics.

Content analysis offers a systematic way to identify patterns and themes in the responses given by participants in focus groups and interviews. Descriptive statistics allow us to use statistical techniques to describe the results of objective knowledge tests and surveys. Figure 13.1 shows which analytical technique is appropriate for the assessment tools.

AN OVERVIEW OF CONTENT ANALYSIS

Content analysis is one method of examining the data gathered from focus groups and interviews. It facilitates the objective analysis of the patterns of words, phrases, concepts, themes, or even sentences and paragraphs contained in the transcripts of focus group and interview sessions. There are two distinct methods of content analysis: classification analysis, which examines documents as a whole; and elemental analysis, which looks at word or word group frequencies. Elemental analysis is usually employed for focus groups and interviews. The overall focus group or interview session theme is already known, because you are the one who designed it. Now you want to look more closely at the results.

Content Analysis	Descriptive Statistics
Open-ended survey questions (Chapter 6)	Single and multiple response survey
Interviews (Chapter 7)	questions (Chapter 6)
Focus groups (Chapter 8)	Objective knowledge test items (Chapter 9)

Figure 13.1. In-Depth Data Analysis Methods for Assessment Tools.

STEPS IN CONTENT ANALYSIS

We will use an example to illustrate the steps you will need to work through in order to conduct a content analysis. For this example we will work with the following questions from the sample interview presented in Chapter 7:

Question 5. How do you feel now when you walk into the library?
Question 6. Can you tell me about the last time you used the library to find information?
Question 7. Would you consider it a successful experience?
Question 8. How did that experience make you feel?

Recall that we asked students these questions and recorded their responses, both in note form and in audio which was later transcribed.

1. Determine What Questions You Want to Answer: Are you interested in how many times respondents said a particular word in response to a certain question, or are you looking more globally at whether responses were negative or positive?

Example: We are interested in whether students had overall negative or positive experiences and if they felt good and confident about their recent experiences.

2. Determine the Object of Analysis Based on the Questions You Want to Answer: Will you be looking for particular words or phrases, ideas, or themes? This can be very simple, such as classifying respondents' phrases as "negative" or "positive," or it may be more complex and require more interpretation, such as determining whether interviewees' responses are related to staff, technology, time, or other resources.

Example: We will be looking for overall positive and negative comments and ideas for improvement.

3. Determine What Will Count as an Occurrence for Each Object of Analysis: Again, if you are interested in specific words or phrases, list them. If you are focusing on ideas or themes, it is important to operationalize your terms so you (or your coders) will recognize the ideas when you see them. This may be simply listing the possible words that might be used in response to a question that represents the idea. For example, if your question is "How do you feel about using library resources?" and you are interested in positive and negative feelings, some potential responses might be "confident, ready to go, excited" (positive) or "nervous, uncertain, lost" (negative). See Figure 13.2 for more positive and negative expressions.

Example: Responses will be coded as negative or positive, with a list of possible responses in both categories included on the coding sheet. We acknowledge that this list is not exhaustive, however, and expect the coders to use judgment when encountering other words. In addition, there may be some responses that are neutral. In the case of multiple ideas within one response, each will be coded separately.

4. Develop a Coding Sheet: After you have decided what you are looking for, develop a form for recording your data. This form may be paper or electronic. The layout of this form should make it very easy to use for coding as well as simple to format

Positive:

Bold	Confident	Happy	Serene
Calm	Cool	In no doubt	Sure
Certain	Courageous	Pleased	Thankful
Clear	Definite	Positive	Upbeat
Clear-cut	Distinct	Relieved	
Composed	Glad	Self assured	

Negative:

Anxious	Indecisive	Tense	Unhappy
Apprehensive	Insecure	Timid	Unsure
Concerned	Lost	Troubled	Upset
Doubtful	Nervous	Uncertain	Uptight
Fearful	Panicky	Unconfident	Vague
Hesitant	Scared	Uneasy	Worried

Figure 13.2. Positive and Negative Expressions for Coding.

for data analysis. If the data are recorded electronically, the coding columns can be inserted in the data sheet. Usually one form is used for each interview or focus group session, depending on the amount of data to be coded.

Example: A coding sheet is created with one row for each subject's responses and the coding of each response.

5. Pre-test Your Coding Sheet: Once you have developed what you feel is a workable form, try it out on a few session transcripts to make sure the form is easy to use, that you are coding the right things, and to determine whether there are things not on the form you want to add. In addition, if others will be coding the transcripts, they should be instructed to use the form and asked to code some of the same sessions. This will give you an idea of how well the form is working and whether you need to train the coders more extensively.

Unless you have too many coders or too much data, you may simply eyeball the work done by coders to determine if they are in agreement. If your pretest generates a large amount of data, or if from your initial examination you are not confident about the rate of agreement, you may want to test it using inter-rater agreement methods. There are several accepted methods for doing this, ranging from the simple to the complex. The method you use depends on the type of data you are analyzing as well as the number of raters. A very helpful Web site on this topic is one compiled by John Uebersax (2003), available at http://ourworld.compuserve.com/homepages/jsuebersax/agree.htm.

Example: The coding sheets are used for a handful of recorded interview sessions and questions are noted on the forms so they may be reviewed later.

6. Examine the Transcripts and Record Responses: Finally you are ready to code the data for actual use and analysis. Although it is recommended that the interviewer, focus group leader, and other interested parties not code the data to protect against bias, you may not have adequate resources to allow you to employ others in this task. If you are able to have others code your data, you do want to check for consistency in use of the form. This is done more easily by assigning more than one person to code several sessions and compare their responses. If you notice large discrepancies you may need to do additional training or revise the coding sheet.

Example: Responses have been coded on the coding sheet as illustrated by Figure 13.3.

7. Analyze Your Data: After all the coding is complete, the data must be formatted so that some basic analysis can be done. If you have coded on paper, the data must now be transferred to an electronic format (usually a spreadsheet). The most common way of reporting content analysis results is by using frequencies and percentages. You may also want to use crosstabs to look at responses across particular demographics or responses to one question in relation to another.

If you are doing a larger-scale assessment or thinking about preparing your results for publication in a refereed journal, it would be wise to present some evidence of inter-rater reliability, as mentioned above in Step 5.

Example: We will look at frequencies and percentages of responses to the four interview questions to determine if students had overall positive or negative feelings. We will examine some individual responses in the coding sheet to better understand the overall percentages. See Figure 13.4.

We can now interpret these results for each of the interview questions.

5. How do you feel now when you walk into the library?
   The majority (8, 89%) of the respondents felt positive overall about coming into the library. Only one respondent had negative responses to this question.
6. Can you tell me about the last time you used the library to find information?
   A slight majority (5, 56%) responded positively to this question, while 4 (44%) were negative.
7. Would you consider it a successful experience?
   Again, a slight majority (5, 56%) were positive about their experiences, while 4 (44%) were negative.
8. How did that experience make you feel?
   Only 3 (33%) responded positively to this question, with 5 (56%) responding negatively and one responding in a neutral manner.

Interestingly, although a great majority of students responded positively to the more general question (5. How do you feel now when you walk into the library?), when asked about a specific experience their feelings were less positive. Examination of the comments reveals that for the most part students feel they have some idea how to get started but know they need help to complete new assignments. The workshop provided the basic introduction but obviously students would need additional, and possibly individual, attention. Some students may not have understood this earlier, which could be causing some frustration.

Questions 5 and 6

Question 5: How do you feel now when you walk into the library?
Question 6: Can you tell me about the last time you used the library to find information?

SUBJECT	Q5 RESPONSES	Q5 CODING	Q6 RESPONSES	Q6 CODING
101	I'm very confident and know I can find what I need.	Positive Positive	I had an assignment for my business writing class and I knew where to go immediately to find what I needed. I got a good grade on the assignment, too!	Positive Positive
102	I'm still a little nervous but think I could find what I need if I take my time.	Negative Positive	I haven't been in to use the library since the workshop. Before that I was really lost.	Negative
103	It's cool!	Positive	Over the weekend I had to do some personal research and I found most of what I needed on my own, but I did ask for some help.	Positive
104	I don't know everything but I know how to get started.	Neutral(?) Positive	I have a term paper for my world music class and I've been coming to the library a couple times a week to get started. Every time I come I seem to be better able to find some useful information.	Neutral Positive
105	Unsure, not confident, still needing help.	Negative Negative Negative	I came in before spring break and it was really crowded at the information desk, and I didn't feel the librarian had enough time to help me.	Neutral(?) Negative
106	It's a great place to find information.	Positive	I don't come to the library very often, but I do check some of the databases from my dorm. Overall I've been able to find what I need for my class projects.	Positive Positive
107	I'm thankful I attended the workshop.	Positive	It was great. I came on a Friday night, hardly anyone was here, and I ended up working with a student in one of my classes. We found a bunch of great stuff.	Positive Positive

| 108 | Glad there is expert help available. | Positive | I came one weekend after work and there was no one there to help me and I didn't find everything I needed. Now I have to go back when someone is there. | Neutral

Negative

Negative |
| 109 | Most of the time I'm okay with the library. | Positive(?) | My last experience wasn't too good because I waited until the day before my paper was due and I was getting frustrated and tired. | Negative

Negative |

Questions 7 and 8

Question 7: Would you consider it a successful experience?
Question 8: How did that experience make you feel?

SUBJECT	Q7 RESPONSES	Q7 CODING	Q8 RESPONSES	Q8 CODING
101	Absolutely!	Positive	Empowered. I would even be able to help other students with simple stuff.	Positive Positive
102	I didn't know what to do or where to go.	Negative	Frightened whenever I get a class assignment requiring library research.	Negative
103	Yes, very successful.	Positive	Happy because I can find things on my own and learn something new when I ask for help.	Positive Positive
104	Mostly successful.	Positive	Overall I felt pretty good about it, but sometimes I get frustrated.	Positive Negative
105	No, I didn't get help and wasn't able to find much for my topic.	Negative Negative	A little worried because I need to get started and I really need more help	Negative Negative
106	Yeah	Positive	Okay	Neutral
107	Oh, yes, very successful.	Positive	I'm very confident	Positive
108	I'd say it was not successful.	Negative	Lost	Negative
109	Not very successful, but it was my fault for waiting too long.	Negative	Panicky	Negative

Figure 13.3. Example of a Coding Sheet for Questions 5 and 6 and for Questions 7 and 8.

SUBJECT:	Q5	Q6	Q7	Q8
101	P	P	P	P
102	P	N	N	N
103	P	P	P	P
104	P	P	P	N
105	N	N	N	N
106	P	P	P	?
107	P	P	P	P
108	P	N	N	N
109	P	N	N	N
	8 P (89%)	5 P (56%)	5 P (56%)	3 P (33%)
	1 N (11%)	4 N (44%)	4 N (44%)	5 N (56%)

P = positive comment
N = negative comment

Figure 13.4. Frequencies and Percentages of Responses.

SOFTWARE TO ASSIST WITH ANALYZING TEXTUAL DATA

Although there are numerous programs for analyzing data from content analysis, we mention only two in this chapter. The first is more useful for smaller amounts of textual data, such as those produced in response to interview questions or open-ended questionnaire items. The second is more appropriate for larger amounts of data, such as responses generated from focus groups. For a review of these and other programs, consult Will Lowe's "Software for Content Analysis—A Review" (http://wcfia.harvard.edu/misc/initiative/identity/publications/content_analysis.pdf). The consulting firm Audience Dialogue also offer more information about other programs for content analysis (www.audiencedialogue.org/soft-cont.html).

SPSS Text Analysis for Surveys (www.spss.com/textanalysis_surveys/)

Many people are familiar with using SPSS for quantitative analysis. The company has recently unveiled a new program that uses natural language processing (NLP) software technologies to analyze survey text (open-ended questionnaire or interview responses). Data can be imported from SPSS for Windows and from Microsoft Excel. The linguistic technologies of SPSS Text Analysis for Surveys automate the coding process, while its manual controls allow you to manage the process and the quality of the results. Results created in SPSS Text Analysis for Surveys can be exported as either categories or dichotomies for further analysis in SPSS or Excel. The program is available for purchase.

CDC EZ-Text (www.cdc.gov/hiv/software/ez-text.htm)

CDC EZ-Text is a software program that helps you create, manage, and analyze semi-structured qualitative data. A response to a question may be entered into EZ-Text either as a verbatim transcript or a summary generated from the interviewer's notes. Data from respondents can be typed directly or copied from word processed documents. Following data entry, you can interactively create online codebooks, apply codes to specific response passages, and export data in a wide array of formats for further analysis with other software programs. The program was developed by the Centers for Disease Control and Prevention and is available as a free download.

AN OVERVIEW OF DESCRIPTIVE STATISTICS

When you collect raw data, you must turn these data into information. You can do that by using statistical methods to analyze and summarize the data. The methods used will depend on the questions to be answered, the type of data collected, and how the data were collected. See Figure 13.5 for descriptions of data based on scale of measurement.

Data analysis may be categorized as descriptive or inferential. Descriptive analyses describe the data only for the group from which they were collected. Inferential analyses involve sampling from a population and statistical significance testing. With inferential analysis we can make statements about the larger population based on the data collected from the sample. Although many individuals use inferential methods incorrectly, often because they want to provide some indication of the "significance" of their results, much of the data we collect when assessing information literacy should be reported with descriptive statistics only. This is certainly true when analyzing data from classroom or one-shot assessments. When working with programmatic or institutional assessments, involving larger groups, longer time frames, and more planning, it is possible to collect data for inferential analyses.

Our focus here is on descriptive methods of data analysis, which require less planning and effort on the part of the librarian. Descriptive statistics are useful for getting a sense of student performance and may help to identify areas for further, more in-depth, study. For example, after determining that fall semester's English composition students are unable to cite sources correctly, you may decide to design a study for the spring semester students in which some receive more instruction in this area. You could then sample from the population of interest, determine whether there is a difference between groups, and perhaps provide evidence that more instruction was worthwhile.

STEPS IN DESCRIPTIVE STATISTICS

We define a five-step process for working with the data you collected through surveys or objective knowledge tests.

1. Get Organized

Your data must be organized before any analyses can occur. The amount of work in this step will depend on the assessment tool and on the method you used to record the data. If you used a Web-based tool to conduct your survey, the data will probably be well-organized and ready for the next step, which is formatting.

If you collected data using paper forms, you will need to spend some time getting the data organized. Start by pulling together the responses to the tools that you used and, when applicable, organizing them into the groups to be analyzed. For example, let's

Data are often classified by the scale of measurement: nominal, ordinal, interval, or ratio. The importance of the scale of measurement is that it determines which statistical techniques may be legitimately employed.

At the <u>nominal</u> level, we group objects or persons into classes so that all those in a single class are equivalent with respect to some attribute or property. No one category has more of a quality than another category—the categories or groups are merely different. Nominal variables are qualitative or categorical. Examples of nominal variables include majors, disciplines, departments, and colleges.

At the <u>ordinal</u> level, the groups of things or persons may be ranked because differing degrees or amounts of an attribute or property may be detected. However, nothing is implied about the magnitude of difference between levels. Examples of ordinal-level variables include professorial rank and student class rank.

Most Likert scales are ordinal in nature. Although we can order "strongly disagree, disagree, agree, strongly agree," it is psychometrically difficult to determine the degree of difference between two adjacent response categories. In practice, however, much of this type of data is treated as interval level in order to analyze in a more sophisticated manner.

The <u>interval</u> level provides a ranking of objects or people with meaningful distance between adjacent score points. Equal differences in the numbers on an interval scale correspond to equal differences in the amounts of the attribute measured. The units of measurement are fixed but the zero point is arbitrary—it does not mean a total absence of the property being measured. Student grade-point average is an example of an interval-level measure.

<u>Ratio</u>-level measures have all the properties of the interval scale in addition to a real zero point, which indicates an absence of whatever is being measured. Because of this true zero, the ratio between measures has meaning. Some examples of ratio measures are the number of hours toward graduation and the number of hours completed in a major.

Figure 13.5. Data Types.

assume that you have given a knowledge test to four classes, two of which received information literacy instruction and the other two did not. You will need to pull together the tests for all students and organize them into two groups: those who received the instruction and those who did not. You should score each student's test before proceeding.

You will also need to organize the rest of the data analysis process at this point. This includes deciding who will do your data entry and the level of your student performance analysis. If you gathered data from a large sample of students using paper tests or surveys, you may wish to have a student assistant do the data entry. This brings up the question of protecting the identity of the students who participated in your testing or survey.

Surveys and even knowledge tests may be filled out anonymously, which avoids the problem of protecting student privacy altogether. Anonymity is common in assessments using surveys. If you are interested in how the classes as a whole did on a knowledge test there is no need to identify the student for that type of tool, either.

If students do provide identifying information such as names or student numbers on the survey or test, then you should protect the identity of those students. One solution is to simply remove student names or numbers from the forms. However, if you are assessing individual performance on a test, you will need to maintain a connection between a particular test and a specific student. In order to keep the student anonymous to your student assistant or others using the data, you can assign each student a number and replace each name on the tool with the student's number. Keep the list of the student number and names separate for your reference when identifying the students and their responses or performance. This process can also be done before any scoring, if you want others to help you score the instrument.

Finally, you will need to decide the level of content that you will be analyzing. In the example above of giving our knowledge test to four classes, you would have to decide how much of the test you want to analyze. Are you only interested in how the classes or individual students performed on the test as a whole, on each section of the test, or on each item of the test? This decision will affect the way in which your data will need to be formatted. See Figure 13.6 for the data organization checklist.

2. Format the Data

Data formatting is perhaps the most important step in the process of working with your data. For some tools and methods, it can be the easiest. Web-based options for some of the tools that we have discussed do a thorough and reliable job of formatting the data that are collected. Many Web-based survey tools not only gather responses, but organize and code them for use in statistical software packages. Many Web-based test and quiz tools do the same, so when working with them, you will be able to spend less time preparing your data and more time analyzing it.

Any of the data gathered using paper instruments will need to be formatted for effective use. This requires the creation of a data file for use in statistical software. You can arrange and enter data directly in the software that you will use for analysis or in a spreadsheet program, saving it in a common file format such as a tab or comma delimited text file. The benefit to using spreadsheet software is its ubiquity. If you are able to get student assistance for data entry, the student may already be familiar with spreadsheet software and may have an easier time entering data. This will create some more work for you when you import the file into your statistical software, but may save a great deal of time on data verification and training.

Formatting your data involves two steps: arranging it and coding it. Your data should first be arranged into rows and columns with each row representing a case and each column representing a variable. A case represents a student who answered a survey or took a knowledge test. The variables reflect each aspect of the assessment that you want to analyze for each student. For surveys, each question would be a variable.

—— Instruments and data gathered and put in order.
—— Decided between analyzing individual and group responses.
—— Respondent privacy is protected.
—— Decided how much of the data will be analyzed.

Figure 13.6. Data Organization Checklist.

For a knowledge test, each item can be a variable, the total score could be the only variable, or both the items and the total score can be variables.

Once you have decided how to arrange your data, you will need to code the variables so that they can be tabulated and analyzed in the statistical software package that you will use. Typically, knowledge test responses are coded 0 for an incorrect response and 1 for a correct response. All other variables will need to be coded numerically using a system that you devise. This is most common for survey responses. If you ask a question on a survey and offer five different responses, each should be coded accordingly (1 for the first response, 2 for the second, and so on). For survey items that allow for multiple responses ("Choose all that apply"), each response should be treated as its own variable and coded with a 0 for not selected and a 1 for selected. See Figure 13.7 for an example of each type of survey question and how it would be coded in your data file.

Each row in Figure 13.7 represents one case, one individual's responses. The second column, labeled Q1, shows responses to an open-ended question, where respondents were able to answer in their own words. (One thing to notice about these responses is how differently people responded to the same question. It might have been useful to pretest this question to develop a set of restricted responses.) The next three columns (Q2, Q3, and Q4) provide data for single response questions with the response options being 1, 2, or 3. The last five columns represent one question that asked respondents to check all that apply. Therefore, the data in each of these columns is filled in if the respondent selected that option and blank if he did not. For example, we can see that the majority of respondents selected the first and fifth options, few selected the second and third, and no one selected the fourth.

3. Verify the Data

Verifying the data means to make sure that the recorded data you have are accurate. Regardless of who formats and enters your data, the data need to be verified before

20: Q1 Open-ended question		Single-response questions			One multiple-response question				
	Q1	Q2	Q3	Q4	Q5R1	Q5R2	Q5R3	Q5R4	Q5R5
1	Geography—urban and social issues	1	1	2					1
2	GEOGRAPHY/URBAN AND ECONOMIC/SOCIAL	2	1	2	1				1
3	(Urban) Geography	1	1	1		1			1
4									
5	Physical Geography	1	1	1	1				1
6	geomorphology of glacial landforms using remote sensing techniques	1	1	1					
7	Department of Geography	2	2	2	1				1
8	Geography	2	2	2	1				1
9	Geography	1	2	2					1
10	Geography	2	3	2	1				1
11	Climatology	2	2	2			1		
12	Geography—Geographic Information Systems	2	2	1	1				
13	Geography, human and cartography	1	1	1	1	1	1		

Figure 13.7. Example of Coded Survey Data.

they are analyzed. The best situation is to have your data entered by a student and verify them yourself. If you do your own data entry, take a break between the two steps.

To verify your quantitative data, start by scanning the data file to make sure that it meets expectations. Does the number of lines (cases) in the data file match the number of students in your sample? Do the values in each column match the available values? If the only valid options for a column are 0 and 1 and you find a few 4's scattered throughout, you will need to closely check the data entry not only for that column, but for the rest of the file against the data you have on paper. A data entry mistake in one column can easily create problems throughout the rest of the columns.

If everything meets expectations, it is still a good idea to do some verification, just to be on the safe side. To do so, flip through your paper instruments, randomly selecting cases. During the data formatting stage, the paper instruments should be kept in the order in which they were entered into the data file, which makes this comparison easier. The Inter-University Consortium for Political and Social Research (ICPSR) (2005) recommends comparing the paper data with the data file carefully for about five to ten percent of your cases as a best practice.

4. Selecting the Right Analysis for Your Questions

You already know what questions you want to answer. You selected and used an assessment tool designed to provide answers to those questions. Maybe you wanted to know what percent of students who completed the course understood a particular concept, so you gave those students an objective test about the concept. Maybe you wanted to know whether classroom faculty value library instruction, so you included questions about that on a survey of faculty. Now that you have collected data, you should review your original questions and determine if you have any new ones that you would like to address with your data analysis.

There are a number of standard statistical procedures used in descriptive statistics, which we will describe below. More sophisticated techniques are available for use with inferential statistics, which is beyond the scope of this book. However, at the end of this section we offer a summary of inferential techniques in Figure 13.8.

Frequencies and percentages may be used to answer questions such as:

• How many students attended the non-mandatory orientations?
• What percent of students who completed the course understood a particular concept?
• How many students answered each test question correctly?
• Which response options were chosen by test takers?
• What is the percent of agreement among faculty about the usefulness of library instruction?

Things to know about frequencies and percentages

A quick way to get overview of responses.
Can pick out one question or item or look at many.
May be used for any type of data that can be sorted and counted.
May be done manually if amount of data is small.

Central tendency and variability are used to answer such questions as:

- How did this class as a whole perform?
- What is the average number of citations in the papers submitted by this group of students?
- What is the most commonly misunderstood concept of the five presented during this session?

Central tendency and variability provide information about where the central point of a distribution of data is located and how spread out the data points are. Measures of central tendency and variability may be used with data at all four levels (see Figure 13.5), but which measures are appropriate for which levels must be determined.

The most common measures of central tendency are mean, median, and mode. The mean is the calculated arithmetic average, and thus it makes most sense to use it to report for interval and ratio level data, which are numeric values. It is often used for ordinal data, however, and as long as you can make sense out of a "2.4" on an ordered scale of 1 to 4 (for example, freshman to senior), it is acceptable to do so. The mean takes into account all scores in the distribution, so it is the most representative measure of central tendency. However, because the mean is most sensitive to outlying data points, it should not be used to describe highly skewed distributions of data. That is, if a few students' responses are very different from the rest, those responses will have a undue effect on the mean which will then convey a distorted picture of the results. For example, suppose you ask students how many hours a week they spend in the library. Most students respond with 10–15 hours, but two students indicate more than 50. Those outlying responses signify that the distribution of data is skewed and that using the mean as a measure of central tendency is not appropriate. Instead, you should use the median (see below).

The measure of variability reported with the mean is the standard deviation, which provides the average distance of all points from the mean and therefore gives you a sense of how similar or varied the responses are. For example, a mean of 70 on a scale from 1 to 100 with a standard deviation of 5 indicates that most people (68%) scored between 65 and 75. If the standard deviation is 20, there is much more variability in the responses, as most people (68%) scored between 50 and 90.

The median is the physical middle point of a distribution, and is the preferred measure of central tendency for skewed distributions (which are most often seen when reporting monetary measures, such as income, salaries, and housing costs). Because it is the data point that falls in the middle of the distribution, the median is less affected by extreme arithmetic values. The median may be used for ordinal, interval, and ratio data; it is more appropriate than the mean for ordinal scores. The standard deviation is the measure of variability used with the median.

The mode, the simplest of the measures of central tendency, is the score or value that occurs most frequently in your data set. It is appropriate for nominal level data, where one is merely counting the frequencies in various unordered categories. It may also be reported for distributions with more than one mode. The range is the best measure of variability to use with the mode.

Things to know about central tendency and variability

These analyses provide two numbers to represent a distribution of data points.
May be used for overall test scores, class grades, or individual exam items.

May be used for any type of data that can be sorted and counted.

Usually obtained using a computer program (spreadsheet or statistical package), although they may be done manually if amount of data is small.

Cross tabulations (crosstabs) are used to compare the frequencies or percentages of responses to one variable with the frequencies or percentages of responses to another. It is helpful if you want to see if there is a difference across groups.

Cross tabulations may be used to answer questions such as:

- How do the responses to one question vary by class rank of the students?
- How do males and females differ in their responses to a particular item?

Things to know about crosstabs

May look at frequencies, percentages, or both.

Provides percentages within and across groups, as well as compared to a total.

May be used for any type of data that can be sorted and counted.

Most easily obtained using a computer program (spreadsheet or statistical package).

Correlation is another descriptive statistic used to determine whether there is a relationship between or among variables and, if so, how they are related in terms of magnitude and direction. Descriptive correlations may be used to answer questions such as:

- Is there a relationship between attendance at a library instruction session and ability to locate journal articles?
- What is the strength of the relationship between class rank and knowledge of library resources?

Things to know about correlation

Provides magnitude and direction of relationship.

Ranges between -1 and $+1$.

Correlations of .4–.6 are considered moderate and correlations of .6–.8 are considered strong.

May be used for any type of data that can be sorted and counted.

Most easily obtained using a computer program (spreadsheet or statistical package).

5. Interpret the Results

The results you obtain need to be interpreted in context, so after you have crunched some numbers you will have to go back to the questions you were trying to answer and look at the results in that light. In addition, results must be presented as part of the whole. For example, if you are interested in percentages, somewhere in your report you must include the total number (n) so that the percentage can be understood as being part of something larger. A case in point: if you report that 66% of your respondents are happy with your instructional session, and the total attendance was three students, presenting percentage alone could be a bit misleading.

Take care to not over-generalize your findings. Unless you have randomly sampled from your population and have checked to see that your sample adequately mirrors your

When we have collected data from a sample and wish to make a statement about the population based on the information in the sample, we use inference. In inferential statistics we conduct significance tests so we can state with a specified level of probability how certain we are of our results. It is possible to obtain statistically significant results that are not really meaningful; therefore, more thought must go into planning research that will involve inference.

Correlation is used as an inferential statistic in addition to being used for descriptive statistics, and the same kinds of questions may be answered. Now, though, we are able to state that the conclusions we make for our sample may be inferred back to the population.

Regression is the flip side of correlation: if two or more variables are related to each other, can one variable be predicted from another variable? An example of a question to be answered using regression is: "Can a student's score on an information literacy exam be predicted based on his GPA?"

The t-test is used to compare means between two groups. You may want to compare the means of two different groups, the same group at two different times (as in a pre- and post-test situation), or your group's mean to some known mean (such as a national test).

Some of the questions that may be answered using the t-test are:
What is the difference between the means of one variable for two different groups?
How does the mean of one group compare to a "known" mean?
What is the difference between the pre- and post-test means of one variable for the same group?
How does the mean of one group compare to the mean of another related group?
Is there an increase in post-test information literacy scores of non-traditional students after completion of a basic introductory session?

Analysis of Variance (ANOVA) is an extension of the t-test in that it compares the means of three or more groups. It makes comparisons between all possible pairs of groups, and provides an overall indication of whether there is a difference in one of those pairings. A significant ANOVA must be followed up with additional tests to indicate exactly which pair(s) of means differ from each other.

The Chi-square (as known as "goodness-of-fit") test is used with nominal data (frequencies, percentages, or proportions) to determine whether the frequencies (or percentages or proportions) observed are different from what would be expected by chance. Chi-square is quite useful for determining how representative our samples are of our populations based on particular demographics of interest. For example, if we are interested in the information literacy skills of all freshmen English composition students and have started with a representative sample to test, if we collect demographics from the sample of test-takers we can compare them using chi-square to the known population's demographics.

Figure 13.8. Inferential Methods.

population, you should not claim that "Forty percent of freshmen have never attended a library orientation" when what you really mean is that 40% of *your respondents* have never attended.

Be certain to report the appropriate statistic. If you are interested in reporting an indicator of typical performance, a quick check of your distribution of scores will inform you whether the mean or median is the most appropriate figure to use. Recall from the discussion of the mean that if the distribution of the data is highly skewed, it is better to report the median than the mean.

Be mindful of including all relevant information. It is helpful to write a brief summary of the questions that were asked, how data were collected, and who the target audience was.

Differences of 1 or 2 points may or may not be relevant. These must be interpreted in context. If you administer a knowledge test of 100 points, the difference between a score of 96 and a score of 94 is negligible. However, if your assessment is five points, the difference between a 5 and a 3 may be more meaningful to you.

Make sure your conclusions are connected to your questions and your overall assessment goal. If you are interested in how satisfied users are with your instructional sessions and some of the responses to your questions are related to library furnishings, you may not immediately use that extraneous information but might keep it on file for another use.

If you notice some trends or relationships in responses to several variables, do not make the assumption that one of the variables causes the other(s) to vary. It is very common for people to infer causality where none exists. In some cases, there may be an unknown variable that affects the known variables similarly. For example, say that you find a connection between numbers of hours spent in the library and success at finding books by call number. You might be tempted to conclude that students who spend more time in the library are better at finding books. One possible intervening variable, however, that could explain that result is whether the responding students are employed in the library. A student shelver or page spends more time than most students in the library and is also more adept at using the call number system. You could exclude those students' responses from your analysis and see if there is still a correlation. Maybe you would discover that nonemployee students who spend more hours in the library are actually less able to use call numbers, in contrast to the original conclusion. The only way to provide evidence of causation is to set up an experimental or quasi-experimental study.

DATA TOOLS

All of the descriptive statistical analyses described above can be run in most common statistical software packages. Selecting the software package to use involves not only the capabilities of the software, but other factors such as software availability, cost, personal experience using a particular package, or the availability of departmental or campus expertise with a particular software package. You may have use for at least two types of software when working with your data, spreadsheet software and statistical software.

Spreadsheets

Spreadsheet software can be useful for organizing and formatting the data that you gather and for organizing your assessment activities. It can also be used for simple tabulations and calculations. The most ubiquitous spreadsheet is Excel, part of the

Microsoft Office suite. Excel is a basic but powerful spreadsheet software and benefits from its prominence. Excel file formats are easily imported into most statistical software and the program itself can import many common statistical software file formats. It is also software with which many users are familiar and can make data formatting and entry manageable for student assistants. Like all spreadsheet software, Excel allows you to perform simple tabulations of the values in your data file and can be used for basic analyses such as frequencies and percentages.

If your campus has a Lotus site license, it may include Lotus 1–2–3, another spreadsheet program. Mac and Linux users can also download the Open Office software suite which includes a spreadsheet program that works well with multiple file formats. Other freeware options exist, but may create more work and complications than they are worth.

Statistical Software

Of all the statistical software available, three packages stand out as good options for the types of analyses described above: SPSS, SAS, and Stata. All three perform the functions described and offer a graphical interface as well as scripting options for expert users. SPSS is perhaps most widely used among librarians and will probably be most easily supported among your colleagues. It is also the only one of these three to offer a content analysis feature for free text, which makes it a good option for qualitative analyses. Note that the SPSS content analysis module is a separate package with an additional cost. Freeware options include stand-alone software as well as statistical plug-ins for existing spreadsheet software, most commonly Microsoft Excel.

CONCLUSION

This chapter provided a very basic introduction to some additional analytical procedures you may find useful in examining the data collected with the tools described in earlier chapters. Two types of procedures were presented, content analysis and descriptive statistics. Some considerations for whether you will use these procedures include the following.

How much data do you have? Our example of content analysis included only nine respondents and four questions. In reality, with so few respondents and a small number of questions, your time would be better spent just reading the comments and hand-tallying the responses. However, if you had 100 respondents it would be difficult to see patterns without making an attempt to quantify the data.

How much detail do you need from the data? If you need a quick read on how students feel about your instruction, a fast perusal of their responses might suffice. If you are planning to make a case to upper administration for more resources and will need to look at the data from a variety of angles, using additional analyses will be helpful.

How much time do you have? If the data you collect will be used to inform another instructional session beginning in an hour, a quick glance may be the best you can do. If you do not need results until the beginning of the next academic term, you may want to spend more time conducting additional analyses.

What level of assessment are you working with? For a classroom-based assessment additional analyses might not be useful, but for programmatic or institution-wide assessment they might be critical.

What is your level of expertise? Even if you do not have experience working with data in this way, if you are adventurous and have access to someone who can provide guidance, you may want to try some of these techniques. However, you must weigh the time you will spend against the benefits to be gained, and determine the right time to call in an expert for help.

WORKS CITED AND FURTHER READING

Audience Dialogue. *Software for content analysis.* Retrieved July 10, 2006 from www.audiencedialogue.org/soft-cont.html.

Inter-University Consortium for Political and Social Research (ICPSR). (2005). *Guide to social science data preparation and archiving: Best practice throughout the data life cycle.* Retrieved July 10, 2006 from www.icpsr.umich.edu/access/dataprep.pdf.

Krippendorff, K. (2004). *Content analysis: An introduction to its methodology* (2nd ed.). Thousand Oaks, CA: Sage.

Lowe, W. (2002). *Software for content analysis—A review.* Retrieved July 10, 2006 from http://wcfia.harvard.edu/misc/initiative/identity/publications/content_analysis.pdf.

Neuendorf, K. (2002). *The content analysis guidebook.* Thousand Oaks, CA: Sage.

Powell, R. R. and Connaway, L. S. (2004). *Basic research methods for librarians* (4th ed.). Westport, CT: Libraries Unlimited.

Stemler, S. (2001). An overview of content analysis. *Practical Assessment, Research & Evaluation, 7*(17). Retrieved March 31, 2006 from http://PAREonline.net/getvn.asp?v=7&n=17.

Uebersax, J. (2003). *Statistical methods for rater agreement.* Retrieved July 10, 2006 from http://ourworld.compuserve.com/homepages/jsuebersax/agree.htm.

14

Working with the Results

Your assessment program will have no impact unless you do something with the results of all of your efforts. Once you have gathered and analyzed the data and interpreted the results, you will be able to demonstrate the impact of your information literacy instruction as well as identify ways to improve. The first step is to share your results with stakeholders in your instructional program. Once you have pulled together all of your results and data to share, the next step is to react to what your assessment results tell you about your instruction, instructional program, and student learning. This chapter will show you how to put your results to work for you.

SHARING ASSESSMENT RESULTS

Identifying Stakeholders

Regardless of whether you analyze your assessment data using the basic methods described for each tool, or the more advanced methods discussed in Chapter 13, your data are useful only if they are shared with your stakeholders. So, you may be asking, who are the stakeholders in your assessment program? Of course, it will vary depending on your situation, but stakeholders typically include colleagues in your information literacy instructional program, faculty colleagues with whom you partnered to provide instruction, library administration, and of course, the students themselves.

Many of the tools that we discussed offer opportunities to provide feedback to students right away. Classroom assessment techniques are specifically designed to offer students feedback and to adjust instruction accordingly, putting the results to work immediately. Scores and feedback on knowledge tests, performance assignments, and portfolios are also shared and provide students with information on how they are doing, and how you assess what they have learned. Of course, self-reflection assessment offers the same opportunities for feedback. Although we commonly offer students immediate feedback regarding their participation in an assessment program, students should also be an audience for more advanced analyses of your assessment data. For example, it is a good idea to make the results of an analysis of survey data available to the students who participated in the survey. They may not look at it or care, but sharing the results with students at least reinforces that their participation is valued.

The most immediate stakeholders in our assessment activities are those who can benefit most from the data that we gather, our instructional colleagues. This starts with our colleagues within the library who provide information literacy instruction through the same program that we have assessed and extends to those faculty colleagues with whom we partnered to provide information literacy instruction and who made their students available for our instructional and assessment efforts.

Although the benefit of sharing assessment results with your colleagues in the library is most evident when assessing at the programmatic level, there is much to be gained by sharing results from any assessment activities. Even if you are assessing one-time instructional sessions within one discipline targeting specific learning outcomes, sharing your experiences and the data that you gathered can only enhance the instructional efforts of your colleagues in even their own specialized settings.

Sharing your results with the classroom faculty with whom you worked is important in at least four ways. It is a gesture that their time and collaboration is valued and that it facilitated the collection of useful data for your instruction. It gives them feedback on their students' performance, knowledge, or affective reactions to your instruction and occasionally to the course as a whole. It demonstrates the value that you bring to their class in particular, and to their curriculum in general. Finally, assessment results can be used to open more dialog with faculty colleagues and provide new opportunities for instruction. It is therefore not only a good idea to share the results of your assessment with the individual faculty members with whom you partnered, but to encourage them to share the results with their colleagues as well.

Perhaps the most obvious stakeholder in your assessment activities is your library administration. Your assessment will provide evidence of what is working and what is not, within your individual instruction or throughout your program. One of the reasons that we assess in the first place is to meet the ever-increasing calls for accountability. Accountability starts within the library and extends to the campus community as a whole. We share assessment results with our administration to not only make the case that our instructional efforts are worthwhile and effective, but to help our administrators do the same among the wider campus community.

Although your approach can change slightly depending on your audience, you can effectively share your assessment results so that any audience can understand what you assessed, how it was assessed, and what you found.

Deciding What to Share

Before you can report on your findings, all of your data analyses and interpretation should be completed. It is then a matter of deciding which results to share, and more importantly, which to feature in your reporting. You should be selective and balanced. Results that indicate that your methods are working, that instructional or programmatic changes are necessary, or that there is a need for more assessment and investigation should be highlighted as key findings of your assessment. Other kinds of results should be included in your full reporting so they are available to those interested in more information.

Selection of which findings to highlight depends in part on your audience. For example, library administrators may be more interested in how many learning outcomes are being met, not necessarily which ones. That type of information is most useful to your instructional colleagues and perhaps to the students in your classrooms. The most basic principle to follow when deciding what to highlight is whether you or your audience will be able to do anything with the information.

Keep in mind that the results that you highlight are likely to be the only ones that your audience retains, so it is important to keep your presentation of results balanced. Results that demonstrate what you are doing well are always easy to share. It is just as important to highlight evidence of areas that need improvement. Your audience may be skeptical of your assessment program if you report only positive results.

Just as you should balance the reporting of positive and negative results, you should include surprising results as well as meaningful and expected findings. For example, if you conducted a survey and found that students are unexpectedly adept at identifying and avoiding plagiarism, you would certainly want to feature that in your reporting. On the other hand, scores on a performance assignment that indicate that students struggle with proper citation of information sources (as described in Chapter 11) may meet your or your stakeholders' expectations, but it is still worth highlighting.

Presenting Your Results

Once you have decided what you will be sharing and featuring, you will have to decide how you will present your results to stakeholders. Will you send a report to them? Post it on the library Web site? Do you have an opportunity to meet with any of your stakeholders? Can you offer a presentation of your results? Regardless of the venue, it is necessary to at least offer a written report of your assessment activities and findings. You may need to put together additional materials such as meeting or presentation handouts and multimedia presentations; however, sharing your results starts with writing the report.

As it will be distributed or referenced in presentations, distributed via e-mail, or posted on the library Web site, the written report should appeal to a broad audience. Like all reporting of your results, it should be selective and make an effort to highlight key findings. You can feature key results through an executive summary and within the larger report.

Writing the Executive Summary

An executive summary is useful for featuring the results of your assessment program. It serves as an introduction to your program, and can also be used to help organize the giving of results in other venues such as in-person presentations. Your comments in a meeting or more formal presentation can be taken from and organized around the executive summary of your report. Unfortunately, it is also the only part of the report that many stakeholders will read. It is therefore important to get as much meaningful information into the executive summary as possible while still only summarizing findings. In other words, balance the need to share information with the need to keep it brief. The executive summary should answer these questions:

- When was the assessment done?
- Who was involved?

- What was assessed?
- How was the assessment done?
- What did the assessment find?

The question of what the assessment found can be answered in a paragraph, but can be more effectively featured in a bulleted list. Even in the executive summary, you will want to offer balance, but it is always good to lead with positive findings. You do not want to bury areas for improvement, but starting by highlighting results that offer evidence of your instructional or programmatic efficacy not only presents your program in a positive light, it helps to keep your audience interested in the rest of the findings by demonstrating that your efforts are getting good results. Everybody likes a winner!

The executive summary should conclude by pointing readers where to go for more information. You might follow the bulleted list of key findings with a reference to the availability of a more complete discussion of findings in the "Results" section of the full report. See Figure 14.1 for an example of an executive summary.

The executive summary should be no more than a page in length. It should be included with the full report and can also be distributed as a presentation or meeting

---

**Assessment of Student Behavior and Attitudes Toward
Citing Information Sources**

Executive Summary

During the 2006 fall semester, 134 undergraduate students participated in an assessment of their behavior and attitudes toward scholarly citations. Each student was enrolled in the English 10002 course at State University, taught by faculty in the Department of English and supplemented by instruction on proper paraphrasing, quotations, and citations from faculty in University Libraries.

To measure student behavior when citing material, students were required to submit copies of each source used when writing the semester-culminating research paper. The research paper assignment was scored using a rubric that included a section evaluating whether sources were appropriately paraphrased, quoted, and cited.

To measure student attitudes toward citing information sources, the same students completed a questionnaire focused on the proper use of paraphrasing, quotations, and citations in scholarly work.

Key findings include:

- A clear majority of participating students used proper mechanics when citing sources.
- Most of the participating students appropriately used citations when quoting material.
- A slight majority of students did not appropriately use citations when paraphrasing material.
- A clear majority expressed confusion about whether to cite paraphrased material.

A full discussion of the findings is available on the University Libraries Web site at http://library.state.edu/assess/citations.pdf.

Figure 14.1. Example of an Effective Executive Summary.

——— Describes when the assessment was done.
——— Describes who was involved.
——— Describes what was assessed and how it was assessed.
——— Includes and highlights key findings in a bulleted list.
——— List of key findings is balanced, but leads with something positive.
——— Provides reference to the availability of full results.

Figure 14.2. Executive Summary Checklist.

handout with the URL of the full report or contact information to obtain it. See Figure 14.2 for a checklist to use when writing the executive summary.

Writing the Full Report

Although we refer to it as a full report of your assessment results, do not be intimidated. In most cases, you will not need to write a very long or in-depth report. The full report should elaborate on the executive summary. Unless you are seeking to publish your results, material typically included in a research report need not be included in your assessment report. For example, there is no need for a review of the literature or much of an introduction. A brief description of your instruction or program and the corresponding learning objectives, and the assessment situation and goals will suffice as the introduction. Although the report is your most complete presentation of results, it should still be kept brief and selective. Do not make the report too much of a time and effort commitment, or it will never get done. It is more important to share what you have learned and organize your results so that they can be put to use, than it is to offer an in-depth discussion of everything that you found.

The organization of your report will depend on your assessment methods. If you used one tool to gather assessment data, you can organize your report around the organization of the tool. For example, if you were reporting on the results of the annotated bibliography it would be easy and effective to organize the report to follow the organization of the scoring rubric, which you not only used to gather your data, but to organize your analysis and interpretation of the data. A report of survey findings could also be organized into the sections of the questionnaire. Even if the assessment instrument is not formally organized into labeled sections, logical arrangement is a key to a well-designed instrument, so it should not be difficult to identify sections of the instrument around which you can organize your report.

If your assessment methods included the use of multiple tools or multiple instruments of the same type (for example, two different performance assignments), organize your report around the elements or section that the instruments or tools have in common. In our executive summary example, the assessment used two tools, a performance assessment and a survey to gather data on behavior and attitudes related to citing information sources. In this case, the instruments are approaching the same topic, but measuring different assessment domains. The research paper assignment gathers data on what students can do and the survey gathers data on student attitudes and perceptions. The two instruments are likely organized in similar ways, or at least gather data on the same topics, so it would be easier and more effective to organize the report into the categories of information gathered by the tools. Any section or topic that is unique to one instrument or the other could be presented in its own section of the report.

When your assessment plan gathers data on diverse learning objectives, or uses divergent tools and instruments, consider organizing your report by those objectives being measured or by the tools that you used. This approach would allow you to extract sections to share for stakeholders interested only in whether your instruction or program is meeting specific learning objectives.

As the executive summary has already highlighted your key findings, the full report should follow one of the organization techniques described above and not push your key findings to the beginning of the report. You will still want to feature important results that are not discussed in the executive summary, or only summarized therein. There are a few techniques that you can use to highlight results within the text of the report: bulleted lists, tables, and graphs.

Bulleted lists can be used to pull out a list of typical responses, common scores, areas of improvement, or other trends that present themselves from the data you gathered. For example, if you designed or used a knowledge test to measure the degree to which students had achieved a series of learning objectives, you could use a bulleted list to present the top five objectives that were met and the top five objectives that remain unmet or largely unmet.

Tables and graphs are useful for pulling out important numbers and statistics. You will want to be careful not to bog your report down with too many numbers, and too much narrative presentation of the numbers can certainly do that. Your narrative can discuss the most significant findings and offer any interpretation of the results; however, a complete presentation of important statistics is most useful in a table or graph. It is important that tables and graphs be used only for presentation purposes and not to offer any interpretation of results. This can be done in the text that introduces or follows the table or graph. Neither tables nor graphs should be used excessively—they are most useful when trying to highlight findings or present comprehensive results. Both tables and graphs should be labeled clearly and use short names and headings. See Figure 14.3 for a table depicting the mean scores on each section of the annotated bibliography assignment from Chapter 11 (see Figure 11.8). See Figure 14.4 for an example of a graph of pre- and post-test results on a knowledge test measuring five sets of information skills.

In addition to presenting and interpreting key findings, the report should provide the reader with at least a preliminary plan for how these findings will be used or have been used within your instruction or program. Options include further assessment, pedagogical or curricular changes, or staffing changes. A full discussion of reacting to the results of your assessment is included in the "Putting Assessment Results to Work" section of this chapter.

Mean Scores on Annotated Bibliography Assignment

	Topic Statement	Authority	Currency	Document	Annotations	Mechanics	Total
Mean Score	3.78	3.39	3.39	3.33	3.78	3.39	20.89

Figure 14.3. Example of a Table.

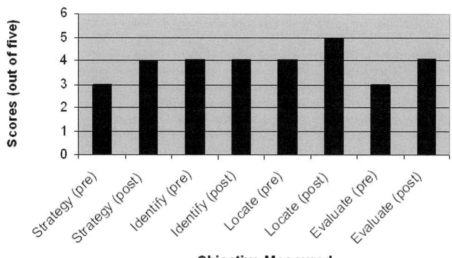

Figure 14.4. Example of a Graph.

To sum up, the assessment report should offer your most complete presentation of results, yet still be brief. It is not a full research report and does not need to include everything you found and represent every analysis you ran or interpretation you made when working with your data. It should be clearly written and organized around the instrument you used or objectives that you assessed. It should also highlight key findings in bulleted lists, tables, or graphs. Interpretation of presented results and a plan for further assessment or pedagogical adjustments should also be included in your report.

Sharing Results in Meetings or Oral Presentations

Although the assessment report gives you a document to discuss with a broad audience, it also serves as a starting point for discussing your findings with more specific groups of stakeholders. You will not need to write a full report for each group; however, you may need to prepare some additional materials to share with specific stakeholders. This usually takes the form of a meeting with the group or a formal presentation of assessment results. Of course, access is a significant factor in sharing results with some stakeholders. You may not have the opportunity to meet with the students who participated to share results. Meeting with faculty colleagues can also be difficult to schedule. In those cases, the report will have to suffice. However, you will probably be able to meet with at least two sets of stakeholders who have a vested interest in seeing and working with the results, your colleagues in information literacy instruction and library administrators. These groups can give you valuable additional feedback on what the results mean and how to react to them.

To effectively present your results in person, use the report as your starting point and select the highlights most relevant to your audience. For example, a meeting with your colleagues in the library may start with the areas of your instruction or program that seem to be most effective as evidenced by your assessment program. To make it most relevant to that audience, you could follow the presentation of your positive results with a group discussion of the approaches that worked in that session or across your program. You will be able to refer to these successful instructional approaches when you present the results that point out potential areas of improvement, following the same approach of presenting the evidence, and discussing why it is that you got these results. In some settings, such as sharing results with your colleagues, it may be fruitful to facilitate some brainstorming regarding the successes and shortcomings of your information literacy program as evidenced by your assessment results.

Regardless of your audience, sharing your findings in meetings or through formal oral presentations will likely require the creation of additional materials. At the very least, a handout of findings and possible next steps is useful, especially in a meeting setting. If you are putting together a formal oral presentation of your results, pull out the highlights from your report most relevant to the audience. You may also find it useful to use multimedia presentation software, such as Microsoft PowerPoint, to create visual aids and organize your remarks. If so, use the same strategies that you used when drafting the report to make it more engaging, less text-heavy, and easy to focus on the featured results. As in any formal presentation, leave time at the end for questions and build in points for audience interaction or discussion. One nice option with using presentation software is that you can distribute a printout of the slides as a good handout. The presentation can also be shared on the library Web site as a more audience-specific summary of the information in your report. Figure 14.5 offers tips for effective presentation of results.

PUTTING ASSESSMENT RESULTS TO WORK

The whole reason we undertake an assessment program is to measure the efficacy of our information literacy instruction and program. We try to answer the question of what impact our instruction has on students. Is their learning experience meeting our objectives for the instructional session or program? Does that have an impact on their overall success on campus? Of course, it is not an easy task to answer these questions. Even a thorough and well-designed assessment program can raise more questions than it answers. Nonetheless, it is best to see what questions we can answer each time we assess and to react according to the answers we are given. In this way, assessment can be seen as a continuous cycle, as illustrated in Figure 14.6.

The cycle embodies what is often referred to as "the culture of assessment," which is of utmost importance to the scholarship of teaching. Ernest Boyer defined the scholarship of teaching in his landmark work, *Scholarship Reconsidered*, where he argued that "pedagogical procedures must be carefully planned, continuously examined, and relate directly to the subject being taught" (1990, p. 23–24). A strong assessment program facilitates all three activities by focusing attention on the continual examination

---

- Extract the featured results in your assessment report that are most relevant to your audience.
- Keep your slides simple.
- Avoid focusing too much on numbers.
- Use bulleted lists, tables, and graphs to highlight findings.
- Provide opportunities for interaction and discussion throughout the presentation.
- Provide time at the end for questions.

Figure 14.5. Tips for Effective Multimedia Presentations of Assessment Results.

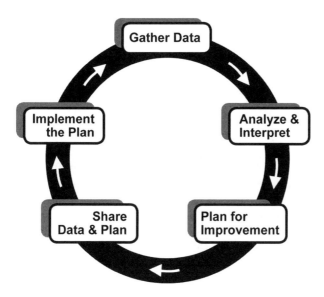

Figure 14.6. The Assessment Cycle.

of instruction and its effectiveness. What it comes down to is, in order to improve our information literacy instruction, we must work with the results of our assessment program.

So, what do we do with the answers that we get from our assessment? It is important to approach assessment results carefully. If our data are truly surprising and not at all in line with expectations, we may want to review the assessment itself before doing anything else with the results. Reexamine the tools that you used to gather your data. Were they appropriate for your setting? If you developed the instrument, is it measuring what you intended? For example, if students used the open-ended questions on your questionnaire to complain about the class or the assignments or even the facilities, there may be something in the instrument that has them sidetracked. Were there any problems during the data gathering? For example, did students have network problems while completing an online questionnaire? Were there any problems when recording or entering the data? A small data entry problem when formatting data can cause significant problems when analyzing it.

Working with Positive Assessment Results

If you have reexamined your assessment methods and are satisfied that the results are indeed accurate, you will have to react to your data accordingly. If you have positive results, your first step is to share the findings. As we have seen in the "Sharing Assessment Results" section of this chapter, you should always lead any presentation of your results with good news. If all you have is good news, share it as well as an examination of it. If your assessment results are accurate and overwhelmingly positive, carefully analyze your pedagogy to identify the approaches that are most effective. If applicable, they can then be used in other settings and to meet other instructional goals. If your pedagogy is not directly applicable, identify aspects that may be of use in other settings. Of course, the only way to know if they have transferred to the new setting or are indeed effective is through assessment. In this case, you would be assessing the same or similar pedagogical approach in a new setting or to meet different goals. You may be able to use the same methods that you used to begin with, or adapt accordingly.

Returning to the assessment process is also an option when you receive good news in your findings. If your assessment results only confirm your suspicions or validate your instructional approach, you may need to expand or revise your methods. In simple terms, you may not be asking enough questions or the right questions about your instruction to identify opportunities for improvement.

Working with Negative Results

If you have examined your assessment methods and are satisfied that your data are accurate and your results identify opportunities for improvement, the first step is to evaluate your personal or programmatic pedagogy. Focus on trying to identify why it does not resonate with your students. Before sharing your results with any other stakeholders, you can brainstorm with your instructional colleagues in the library on what you are doing in your instruction or what you are all doing in your instructional program that does not facilitate student learning. There may be approaches that your colleagues use in sessions that were not assessed, that may prove to be effective once assessed. At the very least, the experience of your colleagues can inform where to look next for answers.

Of course, identifying areas for growth and improvement is a goal of any assessment activity, so negative results should be approached as areas of focus in your pedagogical or programmatic planning and not as any kind of embarrassment. As such, the most important thing that you can do is to plan for changes in your instructional approach. If you do not have new ideas or unique experience among your colleagues in this area, a review of the literature, attending workshops, or participation in discussions with colleagues outside your institution can give you new ideas to use in the classroom. If you have assessed at the programmatic level and identified the need for significant changes in approach, consider making instruction a focus of professional development. You might consult with effective faculty colleagues on campus for pedagogical ideas or invite them to meet with your instructional librarians as part of professional development.

Changing your pedagogy, assignments, or manner in the classroom can increase student learning. Plan to implement one change for the next semester and return to the assessment stage of the cycle. You will not want to change everything at once, unless nothing seems to be working after your first round of assessment. Making one change or a small combination of changes before assessing again gives you increased confidence that the new approach is indeed having an impact.

Returning to the assessment process is also an option when you receive bad news the first time around. You could have just had a bad semester! Even if you are satisfied with the quality of the data gathered by your methods, you may not have used the best tool or instrument the first time around. Assessment again allows you to confirm that you should indeed focus your attention in developing your instruction in the areas that you have identified.

CONCLUSION

Your assessment program will probably identify both strengths and weaknesses of your instruction. You will want to approach your post-assessment planning carefully.

It is important not to de-emphasize those instructional goals that are being met in order to improve in other areas. A careful and thoughtful approach to each stage of the assessment cycle is best. Even if you do identify opportunities for improvement, plan that improvement systematically. You will not be able to fix it all at once, and you do not want to ignore any stage in the assessment cycle for a quick fix. Assessment works best when it is carefully integrated into your instruction or instructional program. It will not be effective if your results are not used or are not used in careful instructional planning. Both your instruction and its assessment will benefit from careful integration and planning, which will also benefit your students and their acquisition of information literacy skills.

WORKS CITED AND FURTHER READING

Boyer, E. L. (1990). *Scholarship reconsidered: Priorities of the professoriate*. Princeton, NJ: Carnegie Foundation.

Cross, P. and Steadman, M. H. (1996). *Classroom research: Implementing the scholarship of teaching*. San Francisco, CA: Jossey-Bass Publishers.

Kreber, C. K. (Ed.). (2001). *Scholarship revisited: Perspectives on the scholarship of teaching*. San Francisco, CA: Jossey-Bass Publishers.

Powell, R. R. and Connaway, L. S. (2004). *Basic research methods for librarians* (4th ed.). Westport, CT: Libraries Unlimited.

Suskie, L. (2004). *Assessing student learning: A common sense guide*. Bolton, MA: Anker Publishing.

Index

About the Authors

CAROLYN J. RADCLIFF is associate professor for Libraries and Media Services at Kent State University. She has a long-standing interest in assessment and library effectiveness. She is a founding member of Project SAILS, for which she currently serves as project administrator, and is co-administrator for the Wisconsin-Ohio Reference Evaluation Program (WOREP). She has published and presented in the areas of information literacy assessment, reference service, and reference assessment. She is book review editor for *Reference and User Services Quarterly* and serves as a manuscript reviewer for *Journal of Academic Librarianship*. She has an M.L.S. and a master of arts in communication, both from Kent State University.

MARY LEE JENSEN is the head of Instructional Services and assistant professor for Libraries and Media Services at Kent State University. She has been in the academic library sector for more than 20 years and has experience in developing and assessing information literacy programs at both the graduate and undergraduate levels. She is a board member of the Institute for Library Information Literacy Education (ILILE) and in that role has focused on high school to college transition issues. Her research interests include the impact of learner-centered teaching, strategies for increasing student motivation, and factors contributing to faculty buy-in for information literacy instruction. Mary Lee received her M.L.S. from Drexel University.

JOSEPH A. SALEM, JR. is Head of Reference and Government Information Services at Kent State University. He is experienced in survey design and analysis and has been involved in a number of assessment activities. At the national level, he chaired the Using Measurement Data for Library Planning and Assessment Committee of the Measurement, Assessment, and Evaluation Section of the Library Administration and Management Association. In 2004 he joined Project SAILS, for which he does item development and testing and data analysis. Joe received his M.L.S. from Kent State University in 1999.

KENNETH J. BURHANNA is Assistant Professor in Libraries and Media Services at Kent State University, where he serves as First Year Experience Librarian. He has experience designing, delivering, and assessing information literacy at all levels of the first year curriculum. He has been active in exploring the role of emerging technologies in information literacy instruction and assessment. He recently published in *College & Undergraduate Libraries* and presented at the Internet Librarian Conference, LOEX, and LOEX-of-the-West. He previously worked as Instructional Design Librarian at Cleveland State University. He received his M.L.S. from Kent State University.

JULIE A. GEDEON is Coordinator of Library Assessment, Kent State University Libraries and Media Services. She is a founding member of Project SAILS, for which she has lead responsibility for measurement and data analysis. She has an M.L.S. and a Ph.D. in evaluation and measurement, both from Kent State. Her dissertation focused on the use of item response theory as a measurement model.